KU-002-281

THE

KITCHEN

SHELF

THE

TAKE A FEW PANTRY ESSENTIALS, ADD TWO INGREDIENTS FROM THE STORE, AND MAKE EVERYDAY EATING EXTRAORDINARY

KITCHEN

SHELF

EVE O'SULLIVAN AND ROSIE REYNOLDS

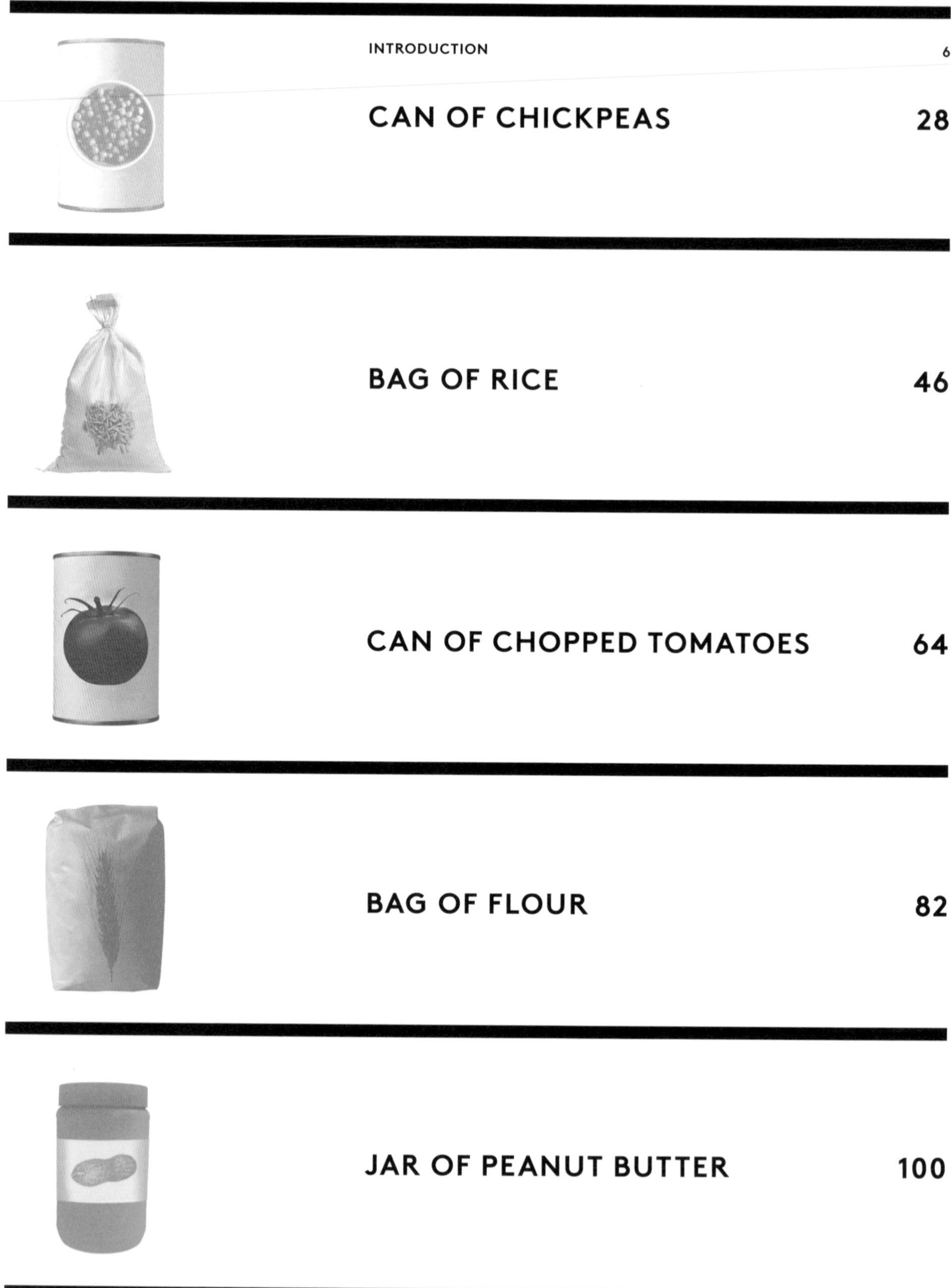

HOW TO HAVE A PERFECTLY STOCKED KITCHEN SHELF

Who doesn't love a kitchen shelf and refrigerator filled to bursting with spreads, jellies, jams, drizzles, glazes, a plethora of vinegars, lovingly sourced cheeses and charcuterie, fruit and vegetables from the farmers' market, not to mention the jars, bottles, and cartons of hard-to-find ingredients from specialist grocery stores and supermarkets?

But the reality is that's not what our pantry and cupboards look like; there are a limited number of good value staples, like a can of tomatoes and a bag of pasta. And our refrigerators, well, the only thing you are guaranteed to find is a carton of milk, maybe a carrot that's seen better days, and a bottle of nail polish, of course.

After years of cooking, eating, and splashing out on "of the moment" ingredients, we have realized that actually, it's all about creating something special without any of the fuss. Those staples on the shelf, supplemented by a compact spice rack and a couple of ingredients from the store, can be used to create something stand out, fail-safe, and most importantly, delicious. And what's more, it's food that reflects modern trends without costing lots of money. It doesn't require advance planning for shopping or take the entire evening to prepare. We think making ordinary food extraordinary is the way forward.

It's as simple as two steps to cook from *The Kitchen Shelf*; stock your shelf (and refrigerator) with the essentials, including easy-to-find dried herbs and spices, then pick up two ingredients from the store and you will be surprised by the variety of meals you can create, from Middle Eastern-style slow-cooked dishes and classic Italian pastas, to speedy salads and show-off bakes.

To cook and eat well every day you need to build confidence and the best way to do that is to master a few dishes that you can tweak to suit your own evolving style. These recipes are smart enough for a dinner party, casual enough for a laid-back lunch, easy and quick enough for a night alone, or perfect packed into your lunch box.

The Kitchen Shelf will hopefully be the start of a new adventure in food; a collection of recipes for you to cook, eat, and enjoy. For the most part they are quick and easy but even when they require a little more cooking time, the method is still simple and approachable. We have given you an equipment list (see pages 23–25), but this is by no means definitive, and you have to work with what you have in your kitchen. There's a lot of merit in learning to improvise—if you don't have an electric whisk, then roll your sleeves up and work on those arm muscles, it just means more cake for you in the long run.

FOLLOW THE RULES THE FIRST TIME, THEN BREAK THEM THE SECOND TIME

WHAT ARE THOSE SHELF ESSENTIALS AND WHY HAVE WE CHOSEN THEM?

The first time you cook from *The Kitchen Shelf*, we urge you to follow the recipes very closely; because we know the recipe will work. When something works the first time, your confidence soars, and, if you like it you will make it again, transforming it from a recipe in a book to a mainstay on your dinner table. Our aim is to build confidence in the kitchen so that you can put your own stamp on our recipes; If you have a can of cannellini beans in the pantry but really fancy the Smoky Red Pepper Dip (see page 31), then swap the chickpeas out and use what you have. The method stays the same, but like-for-like ingredients can change. It's about knowing the recipe will still work and you will be really pleased that you didn't have to make a mad dash to the store for another ingredient! At the beginning of each chapter we have provided a basic recipe with three variations to give you a feel for how easily recipes can be adapted.

In our opinion, of the thirty kitchen shelf essentials there are ten key ingredients that are the heroes of our pantry: chickpeas, canned tomatoes, coconut milk, flour, eggs, pasta, rice, milk, peanut butter, and a bar of chocolate. One or more of these key ingredients will form the basis of all of our recipes, from Coconut and Lime Meringue Pie (see page 168) to Slow-Cooked Leg of Lamb with Moroccan Spices and Chickpeas (see page 40). There is a chapter dedicated to each of these ten kitchen shelf ingredients in this book.

KEY CHAPTER INGREDIENTS:

CAN OF CHICKPEAS

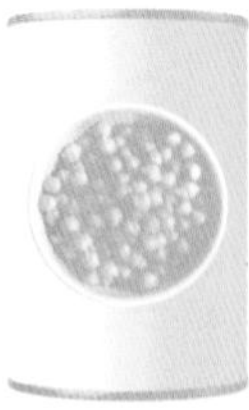

BAG OF RICE

CAN OF CHOPPED TOMATOES

BAG OF FLOUR

JAR OF PEANUT BUTTER

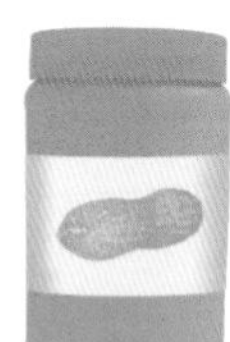

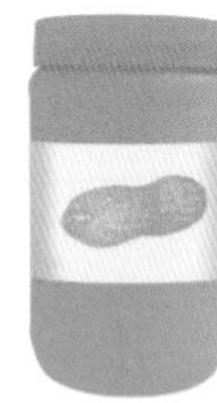

BOX OF EGGS

BAG OF PASTA

CAN OF COCONUT MILK

BAR OF CHOCOLATE

BOTTLE OF MILK

SHELF ESSENTIALS:

SALT	PEPPER	OLIVE OIL	WHITE WINE VINEGAR	BOUILLON (STOCK) CUBES
GROUND TURMERIC	GARLIC	BAKING POWDER	MUSTARD SEEDS	CAN OF ANCHOVIES
THYME	MUSTARD	OREGANO	SOY SAUCE	SUGAR
CUMIN SEEDS	CHILI FLAKES	ONIONS	GROUND CINNAMON	SMOKED PAPRIKA

CAN OF CHICKPEAS

Whether simmered, roasted, fried, or processed to a puree, a can of chickpeas, or garbanzo beans, is one of the most nutritious, versatile, and good value ingredients you can have on the shelf. In this chapter you will find everything from an Indian-spiced salad, such as the Spiced Chickpea and Mackerel Salad (see page 34) to a slow-cooked Moroccan-inspired roast (see page 40), and even Fudgy Chocolate and Marmalade Chickpea Brownies (see page 44).

BAG OF RICE

Normally featuring in a supporting role, rice is actually one of the most versatile kitchen shelf staples, and it's about time it was allowed to shine. You can go to town with rice with a rich and indulgent Rice Pudding (see page 48) just as easily as you can whip up a simple dinner of Greek Spinach Rice with Feta (see page 54). Use white basmati rice.

CAN OF CHOPPED TOMATOES

We simply can't imagine cooking without them. From juicy plum to teeny cherry tomatoes in their rich juices, canned tomatoes form the base of so many of our recipes; adding different combinations of herbs and spices to your canned tomatoes will take you from Italy to Spain, and all the way back to the US and UK via Morocco. A can of chopped tomatoes certainly does go a long way.

BAG OF FLOUR

Rarely is there a cuisine that doesn't use flour, from simple Mini Pecan Pies (see page 91) to Turkish-style pizzas (see pages 84–85). Our Squash Dumplings (see page 92) certainly wouldn't be a dumpling without it and the Blueberry and Cinnamon Clafoutis (see page 98) wouldn't rise and fall, all the while housing sweet berries, if it wasn't for flour. Use all-purpose (plain) flour.

JAR OF PEANUT BUTTER

If more often nut butter is something you consume right from the jar on the end of a spoon or invariably your finger, then you are missing a trick. Swap dairy butter for its nutty counterpart in Peanut Blondies (see page 116), Chocolate and Peanut Butter Fondants (see page 115), and Banana Pancakes with Peanut Butter and Bacon (see page 109). Stir it through noodles with chile and scallions (spring onion), or use it to make brilliant Indonesian-style Chicken Satay (see page 110). We love crunchy peanut butter, but you can use your favorite nut butter in its place if you are not a fan—almond butter works really well as it still has some texture.

BOX OF EGGS

Like most English people, we think putting a fried egg on anything makes it taste better. But, the real reason we love eggs so much is because they work so hard for you. Not only are they the perfect protein hit when hard-boiled in salads, they act as a raising agent in cakes, a thickener in sauces, and produce huge pillowy clouds of meringue. You will never go hungry if you have them in stock.

BAG OF PASTA

A bag of pasta is the perfect food if you only have a pocket full of loose change. Cheap, filling, and ready to eat in less than 20 minutes, pasta has so many guises from speedy weeknight suppers to Saturday night entertaining dishes; there is no ingredient that satisfies in quite the same way. We've used different types of pasta because they suit the sauces, but you can use whatever you have on your shelf.

CAN OF COCONUT MILK

Anyone who assumes coconut milk is only for curries is utterly mistaken. In fact, its uses are as diverse as South American desserts, Vietnamese pancakes, such as the Banh Xeo with Crunchy Cabbage and Soy and Chili Shrimp (see page 163), and Jamaican rice dishes, like Rice and Peas with Spiced Pork Loin Steaks (see page 166). And it's great for a dairy-free diet.

BAR OF CHOCOLATE

Even if you don't have a sweet tooth, we suggest that you always have a bar of chocolate in stock if only for its crowd-pleasing abilities when it comes to quick desserts. We think you will be surprised by how a chili can be transformed with a few squares of bittersweet (dark) chocolate...and how quick and easy it is to make a smooth and silky Chocolate Ganache (see page 174) that can morph into Chocolate and Hazelnut Truffles (see page 175), a Classic Chocolate Tart (see page 174), and small but mighty Rosemary Chocolate Pots (see page 175).

CARTON OF MILK

Not just for your morning coffee; making your own Homemade Ricotta (see page 192) seems like it would be quite a feat but add a spoonful of vinegar to a pan of gently heated milk and watch the magic unfold. You can even roast a whole chicken in it, as in the Chicken Cooked in Milk with Lemon and Garlic (see page 196), making the most delicious nutty sauce and succulent chicken imaginable. We love whole (full-fat) milk for creaminess and taste.

INVEST IN FLAVOR: THE SHELF BASICS

One of the best ways to get lots of flavor into seemingly simple food is using dried herbs and spices, garlic, onions, a pinch of sugar, and a dash of vinegar in your dishes. Alongside the ten key chapter ingredients listed on pages 12–13, you will need to stock your shelf with these twenty basics. You may have some of these on your kitchen shelf already, but if you don't, we ask you to spend a bit—not a lot—of money on the basic ingredients to make your food taste amazing.

CUMIN SEEDS

Used widely in Indian, Turkish, Mexican, and Middle Eastern cooking. Cumin seeds have a distinctive earthy flavor.

MUSTARD SEEDS

Good for pickling, curries, and great as a base in marinades.

GROUND TURMERIC

Essential for color and flavor in authentic Indian dishes.

GROUND CINNAMON

One of the best all-rounders, working brilliantly in both sweet and savory food.

DRIED OREGANO

A natural affinity to tomato sauces, and great in dressings too.

DRIED THYME

Deeply savory, and especially powerful in dried form.

MUSTARD

Adds a piquancy and kick to everything from winter stews to summer salad dressings. We have used whole grain mustard throughout the book.

CHILI FLAKES

Essential for adding heat, and as a little goes a long way, they are much more economical than a fresh chile.

SMOKED PAPRIKA

A staple in Spanish and Mexican cooking and a flavor of which we can't get enough.

GARLIC

There is no cuisine in the world that doesn't use it. And we love it.

BAKING POWDER

There's no need to buy self-rising flour, just add 1 teaspoon baking powder per generous ¾ cup (3½ oz/100 g) all-purpose (plain) flour. It's the only raising agent you need for perfect cakes, cookies, scones, and flatbreads.

OLIVE OIL

It doesn't have to be the best quality, but get something as decent as you can afford.

SUGAR

Not just for the sweet tooth, sugar balances acidity in savory dishes too. Use superfine (caster) sugar.

SOY SAUCE

The source of umami flavor in everything from Italian-style tomato sauce to Southeast Asian marinades.

BOUILLON (STOCK) CUBES

Adds flavor to sauce bases, soups, and stews.

WHITE WINE VINEGAR

Balances out sweetness and keeps your palate interested.

ONIONS

Sweet, sticky, savory, and sharp, onions are the starting point for so many brilliant recipes.

ANCHOVIES

Love them or hate them, they add deep saltiness to savory dishes and when cooked, melt into sauces and joints of meat leaving no trace of fish flavor.

SALT AND PEPPER

The building blocks of flavor; make sure you taste as you go, and add more salt and pepper if you feel it would enliven your dish. Remember you can always add but you can't take away seasoning. We love flaky sea salt and freshly ground black pepper.

TWO INGREDIENTS FROM THE STORE

Who wants to be laden down with bags and a big shopping list after a long day? The thought is enough to drive you into the arms of your local takeout (takeaway), and that's why our recipes will only ever need two ingredients to be bought from the store. A bunch of parsley, a lettuce, an eggplant (aubergine), or even a loaf of bread can go a long way when you mix it with our kitchen shelf essentials.

Hailing from the north and east of England but now living in London, we are aware that although it's easy to find a lot of ingredients in a big city, that's not the case everywhere. The only additional ingredients in this book can be found in your local store, grocery store, or supermarket, meaning that no matter where you are you will be able to cook from *The Kitchen Shelf*.

Look for the shopping basket symbol above the ingredients list to find out what you need to buy from the store.

THIS IS HOW EACH RECIPE WORKS:

KEY CHAPTER INGREDIENT:

SHELF ESSENTIALS:

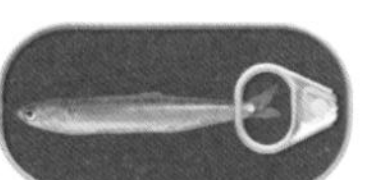

FROM THE STORE:

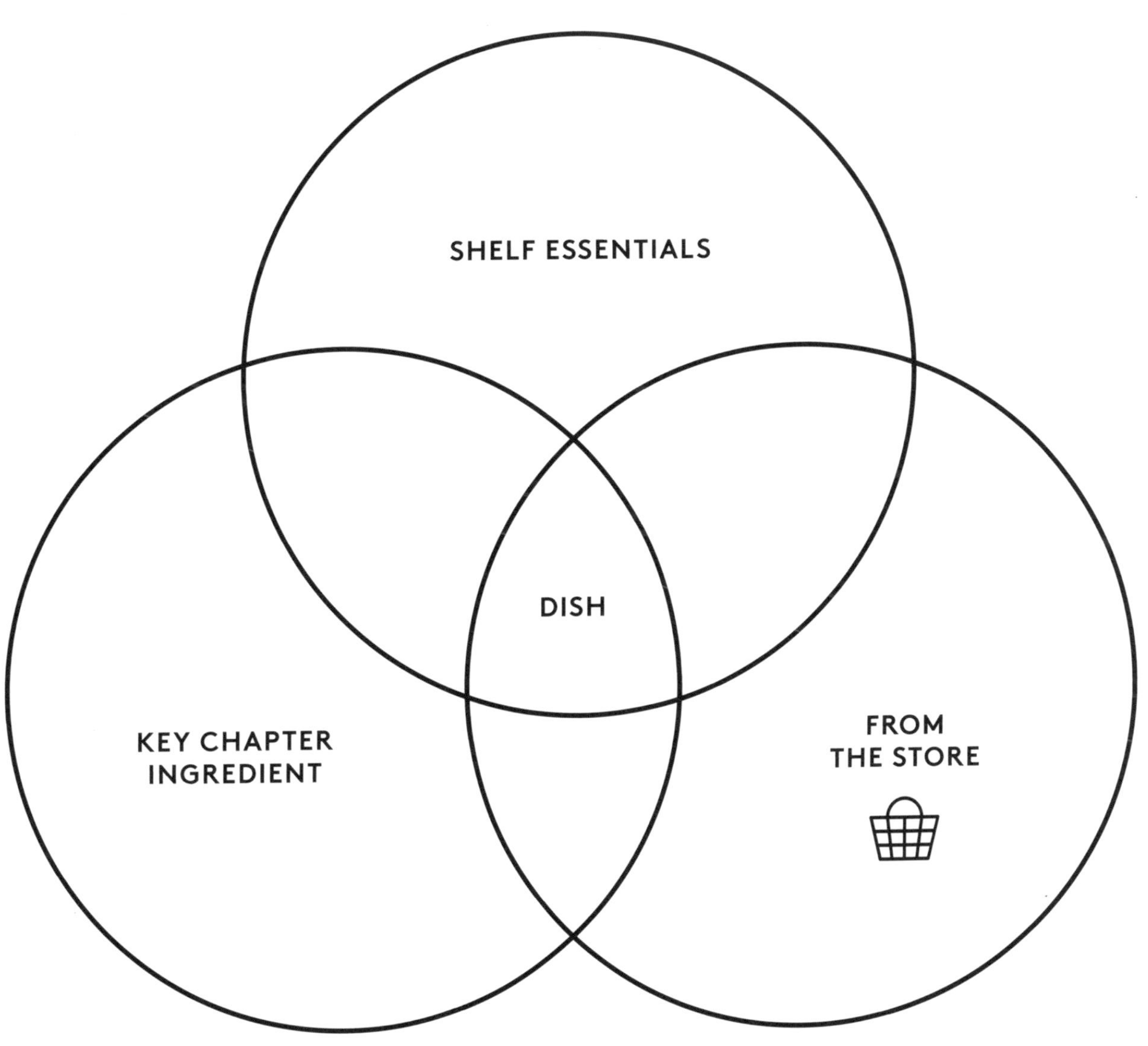
SHELF ESSENTIALS
DISH
KEY CHAPTER INGREDIENT
FROM THE STORE

USEFUL EQUIPMENT

Now that you have got the ingredients, here's a list of equipment you will find useful to make the recipes in this book:

CUTTING (CHOPPING) BOARD

Wooden or plastic, it doesn't have to be anything fancy. Have a few and keep separate ones for fruit and vegetable prep, meat, and bread—it stops flavors transferring. Scrub clean after use with hot soapy water.

NICE SHARP KNIFE FOR CHOPPING

The sharper your knife, the sooner your dinner will be on the table.

SERRATED KNIFE

Much better for cutting fruit and halving cakes.

COUPLE OF MIXING BOWLS

One large and one smaller.

COUPLE OF DIFFERENT SIZED SAUCEPANS

You will need a medium one for stews and soups, and a large one that's big enough to cook pasta in lots of salty water, as well as a couple of small ones.

LARGE NONSTICK SKILLET (FRYING PAN)

A larger skillet will mean you are able to cook bigger batches, reducing over crowding, and so will save you time.

MEASURING PITCHER (JUG)

Essential for baking.

SET OF MEASURING CUPS

If you want to follow the US cup measurements.

SPOONS AND SPATULAS

You will need a wooden spoon, a tablespoon, a couple of teaspoons, and a slotted metal spoon, as well as a spatula (fish slice) for lifting and flipping.

MEASURING SPOONS

They are different beasts to the above if you want a good bake, proper measuring spoons ranging from ¼ teaspoon to 1 tablespoon are essential.

OVENPROOF DISH

Glass, enamel, or tin are all fine.

GRATER

A box grater is the easiest and most versatile.

ROLLING PIN

Makes light work of rolling and shaping Turkish Pide (see page 84).

ROUND COOKIE CUTTERS

For stamping out cookies and scones.

8-INCH (20-CM) LOOSE-BOTTOMED SPRINGFORM CAKE PAN

If you are keen on making cakes, this is ideal.

8-INCH (20-CM) TART PAN OR PIE DISH

Go for fluted for extra prettiness and loose-bottomed for ease.

COUPLE OF BAKING SHEETS

Make sure they aren't too big for your oven.

PARCHMENT (BAKING) PAPER

Will stop your cakes and baked goods sticking to the pan. It also saves on washing up and is actually very pretty (perfect for an Instagram moment).

ELECTRIC WHISK OR A HANDHELD BALLOON WHISK

The former will save you a lot of time.

OVEN THERMOMETER

The temperature on the dial is not always what you think. An oven thermometer is not strictly essential but it will show you what the true temperature is, and save the tears before teatime.

AND FINAL NOTE

A couple of words of advice, and some information about what to buy when using this book.

Get to know your oven; if you are baking, identify any hot spots or cold spots—are your cakes browner on one side? Does the batter peak in the middle and create a dome? If you know how your oven works, you will be more in control of the finished bake. As we have said before, an oven thermometer (see page 25) is helpful for baking.

If a recipe calls for cooked rice and you want to cook, cool, and store the rice yourself, the safest way to do this is to cook the rice as per the package directions, drain the cooked rice then run under ice-cold water until completely cold. Drain again then store in the refrigerator until ready to use. Cold cooked rice should sit happily in the refrigerator for 1–2 days without spoiling.

CAN OF CHICKPEAS

CHICKPEA DIP (BASIC RECIPE)

SERVES 4
PREPARATION TIME: 5 MINUTES

1 × 14-OZ/400-G CAN CHICKPEAS, DRAINED AND RINSED
1 CLOVE GARLIC, CRUSHED
4 TABLESPOONS OLIVE OIL, PLUS EXTRA TO SERVE
SALT AND FRESHLY GROUND BLACK PEPPER

This basic recipe works really well just as it is or you can try the variations that follow.

- Put all the ingredients into a food processor and process until smooth, then check the seasoning. Serve immediately, drizzled with extra oil, or cover and chill until ready to use.

BEET AND CUMIN DIP

FROM THE STORE:
COOKED BEETS (BEETROOTS) IN NATURAL JUICES

1 × CHICKPEA DIP (BASIC RECIPE) INGREDIENTS
3 COOKED BEETS (BEETROOTS) IN NATURAL JUICES, DRAINED
1 TEASPOON TOASTED CUMIN SEEDS, PLUS EXTRA TO SPRINKLE

- Add the beets (beetroots) and cumin seeds to the food processor with the basic recipe ingredients and process until smooth. Drizzle with extra oil and sprinkle with a few extra cumin seeds before serving.

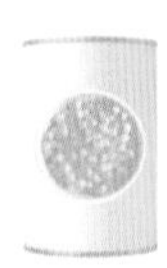

SMOKY RED PEPPER DIP

FROM THE STORE:
ROASTED RED BELL PEPPERS

1 × CHICKPEA DIP (BASIC RECIPE) INGREDIENTS
3 ROASTED RED BELL PEPPERS FROM A JAR, DRAINED AND COARSELY CHOPPED
2 TEASPOONS SMOKED PAPRIKA, PLUS EXTRA TO SPRINKLE

- Add the bell peppers and paprika to the food processor with the basic recipe ingredients and process until smooth. Drizzle with extra oil and sprinkle with extra paprika before serving.

 +     

PEA AND MINT DIP

FROM THE STORE:
FROZEN PEAS
MINT

1 × CHICKPEA DIP (BASIC RECIPE) INGREDIENTS
1⅓ CUPS (5 OZ/150 G) FROZEN PEAS, THAWED AND DRAINED
½ BUNCH MINT, COARSELY CHOPPED, PLUS EXTRA TO SPRINKLE

- Add the peas and mint to the food processor with the basic recipe ingredients and process until smooth. Drizzle with extra oil and sprinkle with some extra chopped mint leaves before serving.

 +     

SPICED CHICKPEA AND MACKEREL SALAD

SERVES 2
PREPARATION TIME: 5 MINUTES
COOKING TIME: 10 MINUTES

FROM THE STORE:
DILL
SMOKED MACKEREL

3 EGGS
1 TABLESPOON OLIVE OIL
2 TEASPOONS GROUND TURMERIC
2 TEASPOONS CUMIN SEEDS
½ TEASPOON CHILI FLAKES
1 ONION, CUT INTO THIN WEDGES
1 × 14-OZ/400-G CAN CHICKPEAS, DRAINED AND RINSED
1 SMALL BUNCH DILL, COARSELY CHOPPED
7-OZ/200-G PACKAGE SMOKED MACKEREL, SKIN REMOVED AND FLAKED
SALT AND FRESHLY GROUND BLACK PEPPER

TIP:
USE HOT SMOKED SALMON FILLETS IF YOU PREFER THEM TO MACKEREL. THIS IS A PERFECT LUNCHBOX FILLER IF YOU HAVE ANY LEFTOVERS.

This is a substantial and comforting dish that is perfect any time of the day. It is also such a simple and delicious meal that it can be easily doubled or trebled at a moment's notice to feed a hungry crowd.

- Cook the eggs in a pan of rapidly boiling water for 6 minutes, drain, and plunge into ice-cold water, then set aside.
- Heat the oil in a skillet (frying pan), add the spices, and cook over medium-high heat for 1 minute, or until fragrant. Add the onion, stir to coat in the spices, and cook for another 2 minutes, or until just starting to soften. Add the chickpeas and cook to heat through, about 2 minutes.
- Shell the eggs and chop them in half. Season the chickpea mix with plenty of salt and pepper, then fold through the dill, mackerel, and eggs. Serve immediately.

SPICY CHICKPEA FRITTERS WITH QUICK PICKLED CUCUMBER SALAD

SERVES 2 AS A MAIN, 4 AS AN APPETIZER OR SMALL PLATE
PREPARATION TIME: 10 MINUTES
COOKING TIME: 15 MINUTES

FROM THE STORE:
CILANTRO (CORIANDER)
CUCUMBER

1 × 14-OZ/400-G CAN CHICKPEAS, DRAINED AND RINSED
1 CLOVE GARLIC
½ ONION, DICED
1 TEASPOON CUMIN SEEDS, BASHED
1 TEASPOON GROUND TURMERIC
½ TEASPOON CHILI FLAKES
½ SMALL BUNCH CILANTRO (CORIANDER), FINELY CHOPPED
1 EGG
GENEROUS ⅓ CUP (2 OZ/50 G) ALL-PURPOSE (PLAIN) FLOUR, PLUS EXTRA FOR DUSTING
½ TEASPOON BAKING POWDER
OLIVE OIL, FOR FRYING
SALT AND FRESHLY GROUND BLACK PEPPER

FOR THE CUCUMBER SALAD
1½ TABLESPOONS WHITE WINE VINEGAR
1 TEASPOON SUPERFINE (CASTER) SUGAR
½ TABLESPOON MUSTARD SEEDS
½ CUCUMBER
½ RED ONION, FINELY SLICED
½ SMALL BUNCH CILANTRO (CORIANDER), FINELY CHOPPED
SALT AND FRESHLY GROUND BLACK PEPPER

TIP:
IF YOU HAVE ANY LEFTOVER FRITTERS, THEY WORK WELL STUFFED INTO A PITA BREAD WITH FRESH CUCUMBER OR LETTUCE, AND MAYONNAISE.

Once you've made these fritters, they will become a go-to cheap and cheerful meal. You can vary the recipe with different herbs and spices, such as cumin and flat-leaf parsley, and serve with a simple tomato salad.

- First, make the cucumber salad. In a bowl, mix the vinegar with the sugar and stir until dissolved, then add the mustard seeds. Peel the cucumber, then use the vegetable peeler to cut the cucumber into strips lengthwise, until you are just left with the seed core. Put the cucumber into a large bowl, add the onion and vinegar mix, and stir together until combined. Season with salt and pepper and set aside.
- To make the fritter mix, put half the chickpeas and the garlic clove into a large bowl and, using a handheld blender, blend to a chunky puree. Add the onion, spices, and seasoning. Stir in the cilantro (coriander), then add the egg, flour, baking powder, and remaining chickpeas. The mix needs to be firm enough to handle, so add a little extra flour, 1 tablespoon at a time, if it's a bit soft. Once mixed, put a little extra flour in a small bowl, then roll the mixture into golf ball-size balls, flatten into disks, then dust in the flour. You should end up with about 8 fritters.
- Heat 1 tablespoon oil in a skillet (frying pan), add the fritters, and fry over medium heat until golden, about 2–3 minutes on each side. Add more oil if the fritters begin to stick. You will need to cook the fritters in 2 batches, so keep the first batch warm in a very low oven while the second batch cooks.
- To serve, mix the chopped cilantro through the cucumber salad, then divide between plates and top with the chickpea fritters.

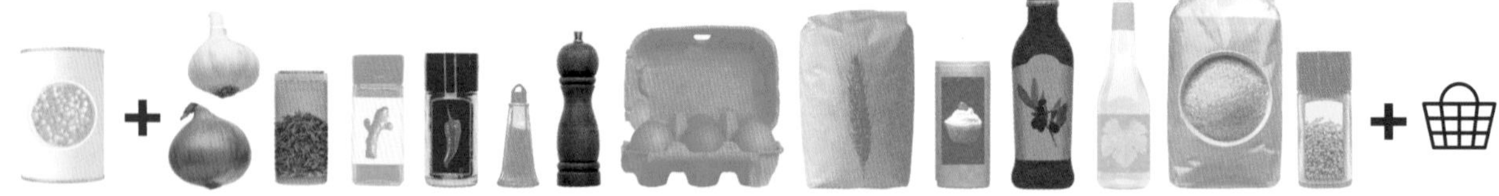

SAUSAGE, CHICKPEA, AND KALE STEW

SERVES 4
PREPARATION TIME: 5 MINUTES
COOKING TIME: 20 MINUTES

FROM THE STORE:
GOOD-QUALITY SAUSAGES
KALE

6 GOOD-QUALITY SAUSAGES, THE MEAT SQUEEZED FROM THE CASING (ITALIAN SAUSAGES WITH FENNEL WORK WELL)
1 ONION, CHOPPED
2 CLOVES GARLIC, CHOPPED
1 TEASPOON CHILI FLAKES
2 × 14-OZ/400-G CAN CHICKPEAS, DRAINED AND RINSED
1 BOUILLON (STOCK) CUBE
1 × 7-OZ/200-G BAG KALE
2 TEASPOONS WHOLE GRAIN MUSTARD
SALT AND FRESHLY GROUND BLACK PEPPER

TIP:
TO MAKE IT VEGETARIAN—FORGET THE SAUSAGES AND INSTEAD ADD 1 FENNEL BULB, CHOPPED AND FRIED IN 1 TABLESPOON OLIVE OIL, AT THE BEGINNING OF THE RECIPE. FOLLOW THE REST OF THE DIRECTIONS, RIGHT.

Blending some of the chickpeas before adding them to the stew makes it thick and creamy. This means that you don't need to add lashings of cream (or calories) to achieve a luxurious taste and texture. If you can't find any sausages you can substitute these for 14 oz/400 g ground (minced) pork.

- Heat a large pan over medium heat, add the sausagemeat, and break it into bite-size pieces with a wooden spoon. Don't worry if it becomes crumbly the sausagemeat will release more flavor. Fry for 3 minutes, or until the sausagemeat is cooked and is starting to take on some color. Add the onion, garlic, and chili flakes to the pan and cook for another 2 minutes.
- Add half a can chickpeas to a food processor and process until smooth. Alternatively, put the chickpeas into a large bowl and mash with a fork. Set aside.
- Put the remaining chickpeas into the pan, crumble in the bouillon (stock) cube, and pour in 3½ cups (27 fl oz/800 ml) boiling water. Stir until the bouillon cube dissolves, then simmer for 10 minutes, or until the chickpeas become very soft. Add the kale and pureed chickpeas with plenty of seasoning and cook for another 5 minutes, or until the kale is very soft. Remove from the heat, stir in the mustard, then ladle into large bowls and serve.

FENNEL, ORANGE, AND CHICKPEA SALAD

SERVES 2
PREPARATION TIME: 10 MINUTES
COOKING TIME: 5 MINUTES

FROM THE STORE:
ORANGE
FENNEL

1 LARGE ORANGE
1 TEASPOON WHOLE GRAIN MUSTARD
½ CLOVE GARLIC, CRUSHED
3 TABLESPOONS OLIVE OIL, PLUS A SPLASH
1 TABLESPOON WHITE WINE VINEGAR
1 ONION, CUT INTO THIN WEDGES
1 × 14-OZ/400-G CAN CHICKPEAS, DRAINED AND RINSED
1 LARGE FENNEL BULB, CORED, FINELY SLICED, AND FRONDS SET ASIDE
SALT AND FRESHLY GROUND BLACK PEPPER
PINCH DRIED CHILI FLAKES, TO SPRINKLE (OPTIONAL)

TIP:
IF YOU'RE HAVING A BARBECUE, CUT THE FENNEL INTO WEDGES LENGTHWISE, BRUSH WITH OIL, THEN CHARGRILL BEFORE MIXING WITH THE OTHER INGREDIENTS.

This light, zingy salad is as good served with broiled (grilled) fish in summer as it is as an elegant but easy appetizer for a winter meal. Saying that, we most often eat it on its own as a quick after-work dinner.

- First, make the dressing. Zest the orange, then remove the white pith and carefully cut out the segments, trying to keep them whole. Put the zest into a small bowl with the mustard and garlic, then squeeze as much juice as possible from the remaining white pith and drain the juice from the cutting (chopping) board into the bowl too. Add the oil and vinegar, then whisk to combine. Add a little seasoning, and check the taste; it should be sweet and slightly sharp.
- Heat a splash of oil in a nonstick skillet (frying pan) over medium heat, add the onion and cook for 2 minutes, or until just starting to cook. You just want to take the rawness from the onion. Add the chickpeas and continue to cook for a minute, or until they are just heated through. Remove from the heat and pour over the dressing. Add plenty of seasoning then allow to stand for a few minutes so that the chickpeas soak up the flavors.
- Toss the thinly sliced fennel through the chickpeas along with the orange segments. Divide between plates and sprinkle with chili flakes for a bit of heat, if you like. Serve.

SLOW-COOKED LEG OF LAMB WITH MOROCCAN SPICES AND CHICKPEAS

SERVES 4–6
PREPARATION TIME: 15 MINUTES
COOKING TIME: 3¾ HOURS, PLUS 15 MINUTES RESTING

FROM THE STORE:
CILANTRO (CORIANDER)
LEG OF LAMB

1 BUNCH CILANTRO (CORIANDER), STEMS AND LEAVES SEPARATED
6 ANCHOVY FILLETS, COARSELY CHOPPED
3 CLOVES GARLIC, CRUSHED
1 TABLESPOON GROUND CINNAMON
1 TEASPOON CUMIN SEEDS
1 TEASPOON SMOKED PAPRIKA
1 TEASPOON CHILI FLAKES
SPLASH OF OLIVE OIL
1 × 4½ LB/2 KG LEG OF LAMB
2 ONIONS, CUT INTO WEDGES THROUGH THE ROOT
1 BOUILLON (STOCK) CUBE MADE UP TO 3½ CUPS (27 FL OZ/800 ML) BROTH (STOCK) WITH BOILING WATER
2 × 14-OZ/400-G CANS CHICKPEAS, DRAINED AND RINSED
SALT AND FRESHLY GROUND BLACK PEPPER

TIP:
ANY LEFTOVER ANCHOVY FILLETS CAN BE PROCESSED IN A FOOD PROCESSOR WITH SOFT HERBS, GARLIC, AND OLIVE OIL TO MAKE SALSA VERDE, AKA GREEN SAUCE, WHICH CAN BE STIRRED THROUGH PASTA OR GRAINS FOR A SPEEDY MEAL.

The joy of this dish is two-fold: First, and most importantly, the taste and texture of the meltingly soft lamb and velvety chickpeas, and second, the fact you will only use one dish in the cooking of a magnificent meal.

- Put the cilantro (coriander) stems, anchovies, garlic, and the spices into a food processor with plenty of salt and pepper and a splash of oil and process until you have a paste. Use a sharp knife to cut small slashes all over the lamb. Rub two-thirds of the paste all over the lamb and into the cuts, then cover the lamb with aluminum foil and set aside while the oven heats. Set the remaining paste aside for later.
- Preheat the oven to 425°F/220°C/Gas mark 7.
- Sit the lamb in a high-sided roasting dish or pan and roast in the hot oven for 45 minutes. Reduce the oven temperature to 300°F/150°C/Gas mark 2. Add the onion wedges to the dish, pour in the broth (stock), cover with foil, then cook for another 3 hours. The lamb should be really tender when tested with a fork. Carefully remove the lamb from the dish and rest for at least 15 minutes, covered with foil to keep it warm.
- Use a large spoon to skim off any visible fat from the surface of the cooking juices in the roasting dish. Tip the chickpeas into the juices along with most of the cilantro leaves and the remaining spice paste, stir to combine, then return to the oven for 15 minutes to heat through.
- Return the lamb to the dish and scatter with the remaining cilantro leaves. Slice or pull the lamb apart with forks and serve with the saucy chickpeas.

SMASHED CHICKPEAS, CRISPY PROSCIUTTO, AND PERFECT POACHED EGGS

SERVES 4
PREPARATION TIME: 10 MINUTES
COOKING TIME: 15 MINUTES

FROM THE STORE:
FLAT-LEAF PARSLEY
PROSCIUTTO (PARMA HAM)

2 × 14-OZ/400-G CAN CHICKPEAS, DRAINED AND RINSED
4 TABLESPOONS OLIVE OIL, PLUS EXTRA FOR DRIZZLING
1 CLOVE GARLIC, CHOPPED
HANDFUL FLAT-LEAF PARSLEY, FINELY CHOPPED
8 SLICES PROSCIUTTO (PARMA HAM)
4 TABLESPOONS WHITE WINE VINEGAR, FOR COOKING
4 EGGS, THE FRESHEST YOU CAN GET
SALT AND FRESHLY GROUND BLACK PEPPER

TIP:
SMASHED CHICKPEAS ARE ALSO DELICIOUS SERVED WITH NACHOS OR CARROT STICKS AS A HEALTHY SNACK, AND ARE A BRILLIANT ALTERNATIVE TO STORE-BOUGHT HUMMUS.

Creamy chickpeas, crispy, salty prosciutto (Parma ham), and soft poached eggs are fancy enough to serve as a smart brunch dish or a light lunch. Poach your eggs following the directions and you are guaranteed to impress yourself and your guests.

- Put the chickpeas, oil, and garlic into a bowl and mash with a fork until the chickpeas are as smooth as you like. Stir in the parsley and plenty of salt and pepper. Set aside.
- Heat a skillet (frying pan) over high heat. When hot, add the prosciutto (Parma ham) and cook for 2–3 minutes, turning halfway through, until crispy and golden. Remove from the heat and keep warm.
- To poach your eggs, bring a large pan of water to a boil. Pour about 1 tablespoon vinegar into a small glass or ramekin, swirl the vinegar around the glass to coat the sides, then pour out the excess and discard. Crack an egg into the glass. Stir the boiling water to create a whirlpool, drop the egg into the center, and cook for 3 minutes (for a runny yolk). Remove the egg with a slotted spoon, drain on paper towels, and keep warm while you cook the remaining eggs.
- To serve, pile a generous amount of smashed chickpeas onto a plate, top with a couple of pieces of crispy prosciutto and a poached egg, drizzle with olive oil, and season with black pepper.

FUDGY CHOCOLATE AND MARMALADE CHICKPEA BROWNIES

MAKES 12
PREPARATION TIME: 10 MINUTES
COOKING TIME: 25–30 MINUTES, PLUS COOLING

FROM THE STORE:
SMOOTH MARMALADE
UNSWEETENED COCOA

- SCANT ½ CUP (3½ FL OZ/100 ML) OLIVE OIL, PLUS EXTRA FOR OILING
- 7 OZ/200 G BITTERSWEET (DARK) CHOCOLATE, CHOPPED
- 1 × 14-OZ/400-G CAN CHICKPEAS, DRAINED AND RINSED
- SCANT 1 CUP (6 OZ/175 G) SUPERFINE (CASTER) SUGAR
- 3 EGGS, LIGHTLY BEATEN
- ½ CUP + 2 TABLESPOONS (2¾ OZ/75 G) ALL-PURPOSE (PLAIN) FLOUR
- ½ TEASPOON BAKING POWDER
- 2 TABLESPOONS UNSWEETENED COCOA
- 3–4 TABLESPOONS SMOOTH MARMALADE

TIP:
SWAP THE MARMALADE FOR RASPBERRY JELLY (JAM) FOR A FLAVOR TWIST.

The beauty of this recipe is its infinite adaptability in a sea of panic-inducing dietary requirements; it works just as well with ground almonds or gluten-free flour if you need to make something for friends with a gluten intolerance, or swap the bittersweet (dark) chocolate for milk chocolate if you're not bothered about it being dairy free.

- Preheat the oven to 350°F/180°C/Gas mark 4 and oil and line an 8 × 12-inch/20 × 30-cm baking pan with parchment (baking) paper.
- Put 5 oz/150 g of the chocolate into a heatproof bowl and set over a pan of gently simmering water, making sure the bottom of the bowl doesn't touch the water. Gently melt the chocolate then remove from the heat and allow to cool slightly.
- Put the chickpeas into a small bowl with the oil and, using a handheld blender, blend until very smooth. Stir in the sugar until fully combined.
- Stir the melted chocolate into the chickpea puree, then gradually add the eggs. Sift the flour, baking powder, and cocoa into a large bowl. Fold in the chocolate chickpea mixture and remaining chocolate. Spoon into the prepared baking pan, then add blobs of marmalade on the top. Using a fork, swirl the marmalade through the top of the mixture, making sure to not properly mix it all in, then bake in the hot oven for 30–35 minutes, or until the brownie is crusted on the outside but still squidgy in the middle. Cool and cut into squares.

 +   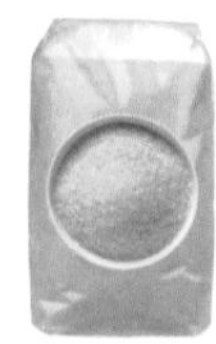 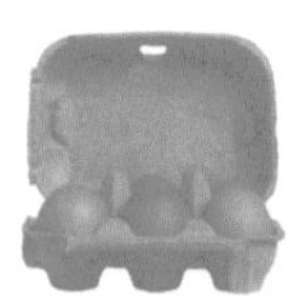   +

BAG OF RICE

RICE PUDDING (BASIC RECIPE)

SERVES 4
PREPARATION TIME: 5 MINUTES, PLUS 10 MINUTES STANDING
COOKING TIME: 20 MINUTES

FROM THE STORE:
EVAPORATED MILK

1 TABLESPOON OLIVE OIL
1 CUP (7 OZ/200 G) WHITE BASMATI RICE
2½ CUPS (20 FL OZ/600 ML) MILK
GENEROUS ⅓ CUP (2¾ OZ/75 G) SUPERFINE (CASTER) SUGAR
1 × 6-OZ/170-G CAN EVAPORATED MILK

You can use any rice for this pudding it really doesn't matter—long grain, basmati, pudding, and even risotto rice will work. Basmati and long grain might take longer to cook so do check the package instructions. Pudding and risotto rice give a more traditional rice pudding texture, a little heavier than basmati and long grain. Experiment with what you have in your pantry. If you have a load of near-empty bags, mix it up—just keep testing the grains during cooking to ensure the rice is soft.

- Heat the oil in a large high-sided skillet (frying pan), add the rice, stir to coat in the oil, and cook over medium heat for 1 minute, stirring constantly. Gradually add the milk and sugar and continue to stir for 2 minutes, or until the sugar has dissolved. Bring the mixture to a boil, reduce the heat, and simmer for 10–12 minutes until the rice is tender and most of the milk has been absorbed. Remove from the heat, stir in the evaporated milk, cover with a lid, and let stand for 10 minutes.

 +    +

RICE PUDDING WITH CINNAMON SYRUP AND PISTACHIOS

FROM THE STORE:
EVAPORATED MILK
PISTACHIOS

1 × RICE PUDDING (BASIC RECIPE) INGREDIENTS
¼ CUP (2 OZ/50 G) SUPERFINE (CASTER) SUGAR
1½ TEASPOONS GROUND CINNAMON
½ CUP (2¾ OZ/75 G) CHOPPED PISTACHIOS, ROASTED, TO SERVE

- Follow the basic recipe for rice pudding (see above).
- While the rice pudding is standing, make a cinnamon syrup. Put the sugar, cinnamon, and 5 tablespoons (2½ fl oz/75 ml) water into a small pan set over medium heat and stir until the sugar dissolves. Once the sugar has dissolved, increase the heat and boil for 5 minutes, or until the mixture has reduced slightly and is syrupy. Remove the pan from the heat and cool for 3–5 minutes. Spoon the rice pudding into bowls. Pour a little cinnamon syrup over each portion and sprinkle with the chopped, roasted pistachios.

RICE PUDDING BRÛLÉE

FROM THE STORE:
EVAPORATED MILK

1 × RICE PUDDING (BASIC RECIPE) INGREDIENTS
4 TABLESPOONS SUPERFINE (CASTER) SUGAR

- Follow the basic recipe for rice pudding (opposite).
- While the rice pudding is standing, preheat the broiler (grill) to high. Divide the rice pudding among 4 ramekins, smooth the surface, and let cool to room temperature. This will take about 20 minutes. Sprinkle each ramekin with 1 tablespoon sugar, then flash under the hot broiler for 1–2 minutes, or until dark golden and bubbling, or use a blowtorch. Cool for about 10 minutes in the refrigerator to set the sugar before serving.

 +  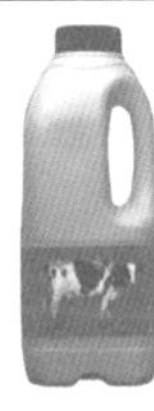 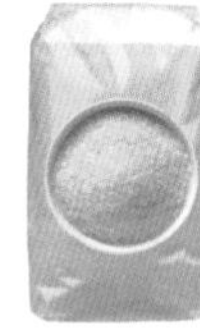 +

RICE PUDDING WITH CARAMEL PEACHES

FROM THE STORE:
EVAPORATED MILK
PEACHES

1 × RICE PUDDING (BASIC RECIPE) INGREDIENTS
1 TABLESPOON OLIVE OIL
2 RIPE PEACHES, QUARTERED AND PITTED
2 TABLESPOONS SUPERFINE (CASTER) SUGAR

- Follow the basic recipe for rice pudding (opposite).
- Heat the oil in a large skillet (frying pan), add the peaches, then sprinkle over the sugar and a splash of water. Bubble over high heat for a few minutes for the sauce to caramelize, shaking the skillet every now and again to dissolve the sugar. Remove the skillet from the heat and spoon the peaches and any pan juices over the rice pudding. Serve.

 +    +

PERSIAN LAMB AND POMEGRANATE RICE

SERVES 2
PREPARATION TIME: 10 MINUTES
COOKING TIME: 15 MINUTES

FROM THE STORE:
GROUND (MINCED) LAMB
POMEGRANATE SEEDS

2 TABLESPOONS OLIVE OIL
7 TABLESPOONS ALL-PURPOSE (PLAIN) FLOUR
1 ONION, ½ CHOPPED, ½ VERY THINLY SLICED
7 OZ/200 G GROUND (MINCED) LAMB
2 CLOVES GARLIC, CHOPPED
2 TEASPOONS GROUND CINNAMON
2 TEASPOONS CUMIN SEEDS, BASHED
1½ CUPS (9 OZ/250 G) WHITE BASMATI COOKED RICE
3½ OZ/100 G POMEGRANATE SEEDS
SALT AND FRESHLY GROUND BLACK PEPPER

The pop of freshness from the pomegranate seeds brings the rich, spiced lamb to life. Minus the fruit, this dish also freezes really well.

- Heat the oil in a large skillet (frying pan) over high heat. Put the flour on a plate, then toss the sliced onion in the flour, shaking off any excess, and put the onion into the hot oil. Fry for 2–3 minutes, moving the onion around the skillet frequently until golden and crisp—you might have to do this in batches. Drain on paper towels and set aside.
- Wipe out the skillet with paper towels and then return the pan to the heat. Add the chopped onion, lamb, and plenty of seasoning, then fry for 5 minutes, or until the lamb is crisp and golden and the onion is soft. Throw in the garlic, cinnamon, and cumin and stir until combined and the spices are becoming fragrant, add the rice and continue to fry, stirring frequently, for 5 minutes, or until it is heated through and piping hot.
- Divide between plates and sprinkle over the pomegranate seeds and the crispy fried onion.

CHEESE AND CHIVE ARANCINI

MAKES 16 ARANCINI
PREPARATION TIME: 10 MINUTES
COOKING TIME: 55 MINUTES, PLUS COOLING

FROM THE STORE:
CHIVES
ITALIAN PARMESAN CHEESE

GENEROUS ¾ CUP (5 OZ/150 G) COOKED WHITE BASMATI RICE
½ BOUILLON (STOCK) CUBE, CRUMBLED
3 TABLESPOONS FINELY CHOPPED CHIVES
1 EGG, LIGHTLY BEATEN
1 OZ/25 G ITALIAN PARMESAN CHEESE, VERY FINELY GRATED, PLUS EXTRA TO SERVE
OLIVE OIL, FOR FRYING AND OILING

FOR THE SPICY TOMATO CHUTNEY
2 TABLESPOONS WHITE WINE VINEGAR
2 TABLESPOONS SUPERFINE (CASTER) SUGAR
1 TABLESPOON OLIVE OIL
½ TEASPOON CHILLI FLAKES
1 TEASPOON CUMIN SEEDS, BASHED
2 CLOVES GARLIC, CHOPPED
1 × 14-OZ/400-G CAN CHOPPED TOMATOES

TIP:
IF YOU HAVE ODDS AND ENDS OF CHEESE IN THE REFRIGERATOR, YOU CAN USE A MIXTURE, JUST CHECK THE SEASONING AS SOME CHEESE IS SALTIER THAN OTHERS.

These arancini can be made small, as the recipe outlines, and served as an accompaniment to drinks or made as big as a burger patty, served in crisp lettuce leaves and dunked into a sweet chili sauce as a tasty alternative to a burger in a bun.

- Make the chutney first: Put all of the chutney ingredients into a small pan and bring to a boil. Reduce the heat and simmer for 20 minutes, stirring frequently, until thick and reduced. Remove from the heat and allow to cool to room temperature.
- To make the arancini, put the rice into a large nonstick skillet (frying pan) with the bouillon (stock) cube and cover with boiling water so that the water comes to ½ inch/1 cm above the surface of the rice. Bring to a boil and cook for 8 minutes, stirring a couple times during this period. Once the rice is tender, stir continuously until all of the water has been absorbed and the rice is really sticky and clumping together. Remove from the heat and allow to cool enough for you to touch the rice.
- Once cool, scrape the rice out into a mixing bowl and add the chives, egg, and Parmesan. Use your hands to mix everything together, squeezing the mix to squash the rice grains and bring the ingredients together.
- Preheat the oven to 425°F/220°C/Gas mark 7 and lightly oil a baking sheet. Use a little more oil to oil your hands and pull off slightly smaller than ping-pong-sized balls of rice mixture with your fingers. Roll them between your hands to make neat balls. Set aside on the prepared sheet. Sprinkle each arancini with a little of the extra Parmesan. Transfer to the hot oven and cook for 25 minutes, or until the outside of the arancini is light golden and crisp. Serve with the spicy chutney.

GREEK SPINACH RICE WITH FETA

SERVES 2
PREPARATION TIME: 5 MINUTES
COOKING TIME: 25 MINUTES

FROM THE STORE:
SPINACH
FETA CHEESE

2 TABLESPOONS OLIVE OIL, PLUS EXTRA TO DRIZZLE (OPTIONAL)
2 SMALL CLOVES GARLIC, THINLY SLICED
1 LB 2 OZ/500 G SPINACH, WASHED
¾ CUP (5 OZ/150 G) WHITE BASMATI RICE
7 OZ/200 G FETA CHEESE, CRUMBLED
1 TEASPOON CHILI FLAKES (OPTIONAL)
SALT AND FRESHLY GROUND BLACK PEPPER

TIP:
IF YOU DON'T FANCY CRUMBLED FETA TRY A POACHED EGG OR EVEN BROILED (GRILLED) CHICKEN AS A SUBSTITUTE.

This meal is so unbelievably simple that you'll wonder how you coped on a lazy weeknight without it. It's great with rice, but you could try it with other grains, such as pearl barley or even pinhead oats. It also works really well with orzo.

- Heat the oil in a large pan, add the garlic, and cook over medium heat for 2 minutes, or until fragrant and softened.
- Add the spinach, a handful at a time, and cook for 5 minutes until just wilted, then reduce the heat to very low and put the rice on top. Cover with a lid and leave for 15–20 minutes; the rice will cook in the water released from the spinach, but check a couple of times to make sure the leaves aren't sticking to the bottom of the pan. If they are sticking, reduce the heat and add a splash of water.
- Once the rice is cooked, season to taste, then divide between 2 plates and top with the feta, a sprinkling of chili flakes, if using, a little black pepper, and a dash more oil, if you like.

PORK SIDE WITH EGG-FRIED RICE AND STICKY DIPPING SAUCE

SERVES 6
PREPARATION TIME: 10 MINUTES
COOKING TIME: 3½ HOURS

FROM THE STORE:
PORK SIDE (BELLY)
SUGAR SNAP PEAS

4½ LB/2 KG PORK SIDE (BELLY), SKIN SCORED
OLIVE OIL, FOR RUBBING
SALT AND FRESHLY GROUND BLACK PEPPER

FOR THE RICE

1½ CUPS (11 OZ/300 G) WHITE BASMATI RICE
1 × 7-OZ/200-G BAG SUGAR SNAP PEAS, SHREDDED
3 EGGS
1 TEASPOON SUPERFINE (CASTER) SUGAR
1 TABLESPOON OLIVE OIL
1 ONION, FINELY CHOPPED
2 CLOVES GARLIC, FINELY CHOPPED
SALT AND FRESHLY GROUND BLACK PEPPER

FOR THE DIPPING SAUCE

4 TABLESPOONS SOY SAUCE
4 TABLESPOONS SUPERFINE (CASTER) SUGAR
1 TEASPOON CHILI FLAKES

TIP:
SHRED ANY LEFTOVER MEAT AND PUT IT IN A BAGUETTE WITH SHREDDED CUCUMBER OR SCALLIONS (SPRING ONIONS).

Pork side (belly) is the ultimate feed-a-crowd dish; no other meat is quite as cheap, easy, and indulgent.

- Preheat the oven to 425°F/220°C/Gas mark 7.
- Put the pork into a roasting pan, on a wire rack, if you have one, but don't worry if not. Rub the pork with a little oil and season generously with salt and pepper. Cook the pork in the hot oven for 30 minutes, then remove, and pour scant ½ cup (3½ fl oz/100 ml) water into the pan around the meat. Reduce the oven temperature to 325°F/160°C/Gas mark 3 and return the pan to the oven for another 2½ hours. During this time remove, baste again, and top up with a drop more water if the pan looks like it is drying out. At the end of cooking the meat, if the crackling is not crisp enough for your liking, put it under a hot broiler (grill), until crisp, but be sure to keep an eye on it.
- Meanwhile, cook the rice in a large pan of boiling water for 8–10 minutes, or according to the package directions, until tender, then drain and cool.
- Remove the meat from the oven, transfer to a cutting (chopping) board, cover loosely with aluminum foil, and allow to rest for 20 minutes.
- To make the dipping sauce, put the soy sauce, sugar, and chili flakes into a small pan with ¼ cup (2 fl oz/60 ml) water. Heat gently until the sugar has dissolved, then increase the heat and let boil for 3 minutes until slightly syrupy. Remove from the heat and set aside.
- To make the rice, cook the sugar snap peas in a pan of boiling salted water for 2 minutes, drain, and cool under cold water. Drain again and set aside.
- Beat the eggs in a bowl, season with salt and pepper, and add the sugar.
- Heat a wok or skillet (frying pan) over high heat. When hot, add a little oil, then add the onion and cook for 5 minutes, stirring frequently, until beginning to soften. Stir in the garlic and cook for another minute. Tip in the rice and stir-fry for 3 minutes, or until piping hot. Move the rice to one side of the wok and add the beaten eggs, tipping the wok so that the egg is over the heat and gently scrambling. When almost cooked, mix the rice and egg together. Tip in the sugar snap peas and cook for 2–3 minutes until hot.
- Cut the pork into thick slices and serve with the egg-fried rice and small bowls of dipping sauce to dunk the pork into.

KEDGEREE

SERVES 2
PREPARATION TIME: 10 MINUTES
COOKING TIME: 30 MINUTES

FROM THE STORE:

SMOKED HADDOCK FILLETS
FLAT-LEAF PARSLEY

9 OZ/250 G SMOKED HADDOCK FILLETS
1 TABLESPOON OLIVE OIL
2 TEASPOONS CUMIN SEEDS
1 TEASPOON MUSTARD SEEDS
2 TEASPOONS GROUND TURMERIC
½ TEASPOON CHILI FLAKES
1 ONION, THINLY SLICED
1 CLOVE GARLIC, CHOPPED
1 CUP (7 OZ/200 G) WHITE BASMATI RICE
1 BOUILLON (STOCK) CUBE
1 EGG
LARGE BUNCH FLAT-LEAF PARSLEY, LEAVES PICKED
SALT AND FRESHLY GROUND BLACK PEPPER

Traditionally a British colonial breakfast dish, we also like to eat this for dinner on winter nights when only something warming and hearty will do.

- Put the haddock on a microwavable plate, add 1 tablespoon water, cover with plastic wrap (clingfilm), and microwave for 3 minutes. Remove the plastic wrap, flake the fish, and discard any bones and skin. Alternatively, pre-heat an oven to 350°F/180°C/Gas mark 4. Sit the fish in an ovenproof baking dish and cook for 10 minutes, or until just cooked, and then flake the flesh, discarding any skin and bones. Set aside.
- Heat the oil in a high-sided skillet (frying pan) with a lid, add the cumin and mustard seeds, and cook over medium heat for 2 minutes until the seeds start to pop and are fragrant. Add the turmeric, chili flakes, onion, and garlic and fry for another 2 minutes. Stir in the rice and pour in 1⅔ cups (14 fl oz/400 ml) boiling water. Crumble in the bouillon (stock) cube and stir to combine. Put the lid on, bring to a boil, then reduce the heat and simmer for 10 minutes. Turn off the heat and leave to stand for 10 minutes—don't lift the lid during this time.
- Meanwhile, cook the egg in a pan of boiling water for 6 minutes. Drain and cool under cold water. Shell the egg and chop into eighths.
- Fluff up the rice with a fork and fold through the flaked haddock, egg, and parsley. Season and serve.

COCONUT RICE WITH SALMON AND CILANTRO SAUCE

SERVES 4
PREPARATION TIME: 5 MINUTES
COOKING TIME: 30–35 MINUTES

FROM THE STORE:
SALMON FILLETS
CILANTRO (CORIANDER)

1 TABLESPOON OLIVE OIL
1 ONION, DICED
1 CLOVE GARLIC, FINELY CHOPPED
1½ CUPS (11 OZ/300 G) WHITE BASMATI RICE, WASHED
1 × 14-OZ/400-G CAN COCONUT MILK
½ TEASPOON SUPERFINE (CASTER) SUGAR
4 SALMON FILLETS, SKIN STILL ON
SALT AND FRESHLY GROUND BLACK PEPPER

FOR THE CILANTRO (CORIANDER) SAUCE
1½ TABLESPOONS SUPERFINE (CASTER) SUGAR
½ TEASPOON SALT
½ TEASPOON CHILI FLAKES, PLUS EXTRA TO SERVE
1 LARGE BUNCH CILANTRO (CORIANDER), COARSELY CHOPPED

TIP:
YOU CAN REPLACE SALMON WITH ANY FIRM WHITE FISH, OR TRY SERVING WITH SOME FRIED CUBES OF TOFU FOR A VEGAN FEAST.

Creamy and satisfying, the rice, crisp-skinned salmon, and fragrant cilantro (coriander) sauce are smart enough for guests but easy enough to whip up after work. You can steam the salmon on top of the rice for a simple one-pot dish for extra ease.

- Heat the oil in a large lidded pan, add the onion, and cook over medium heat for 10 minutes, or until softened. Add the garlic and cook for 1–2 minutes, until fragrant, then tip in the rice and stir to coat in the oil. Add the coconut milk, then half fill the empty coconut milk can with water and pour into the pan. Add a generous pinch of salt and the sugar, bring to a boil, then reduce the heat to a simmer. Cook for 10 minutes, or until the rice is just tender and the liquid has been absorbed.
- Season the salmon fillets with salt and pepper. Heat a large nonstick skillet (frying pan) over medium–high heat, place the fillets in the skillet skin-side down, and cook for 3 minutes, or until the skin is golden and crisp. Flip the fillets over and cook for another 2 minutes. Remove from the skillet and keep warm. Alternatively, you can place the salmon fillets on top of the rice, cover with the lid, and cook for 10 minutes until the fish and the rice are just cooked.
- To make the cilantro (coriander) sauce, pour scant ½ cup (3½ fl oz/100 ml) water into a small pan, add the sugar, salt, and chili flakes, and bring to a boil. Simmer for 3–5 minutes, or until slightly reduced and syrupy. Remove from the heat.
- Put the cilantro into a food processor and pulse to chop. Gradually pour in the syrup and continue to pulse until the cilantro is finely chopped and the sauce is combined. Check the seasoning; it should be slightly sweet with a hint of chili.
- To serve, divide the rice and fish among 4 plates, then drizzle generously with the sauce and sprinkle with extra chili flakes, if you like.

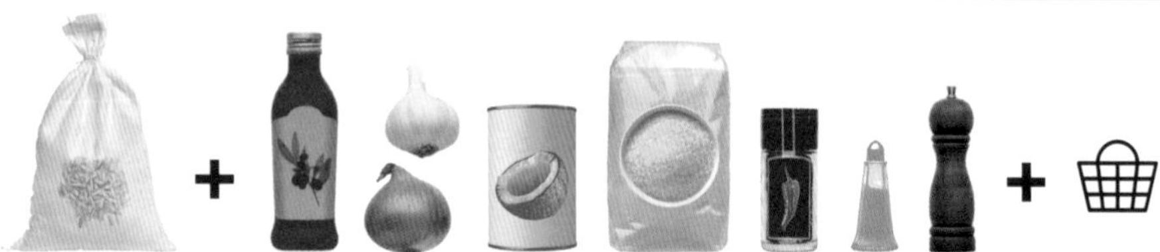

MEXICAN CHICKEN, CHICKPEA, AND RICE BOWLS WITH PICKLED ONIONS AND AVOCADO CREAM

SERVES 4
PREPARATION TIME: 15 MINUTES
COOKING TIME: 45 MINUTES

FROM THE STORE:
CHICKEN THIGHS
AVOCADO

1 TABLESPOON OLIVE OIL
4 CHICKEN THIGHS, SKIN ON AND BONE IN
2 ONIONS, FINELY CHOPPED
2 CLOVES GARLIC, CHOPPED
2 TEASPOONS SMOKED PAPRIKA
1 TEASPOON CHILI FLAKES
1 TEASPOON GROUND CINNAMON
2 TEASPOONS CUMIN SEEDS, BASHED
1 CUP (7 OZ/200 G) WHITE BASMATI RICE
1 × 14-OZ/400-G CAN CHICKPEAS, DRAINED AND RINSED
1 × 14-OZ/400-G CAN CHOPPED TOMATOES
1 BOUILLON (STOCK) CUBE
1 TABLESPOON WHITE WINE VINEGAR
½ TEASPOON SUPERFINE (CASTER) SUGAR
SALT AND FRESHLY GROUND BLACK PEPPER

FOR THE AVOCADO CREAM
1 AVOCADO, HALVED, PEELED, AND PITTED
½ CLOVE GARLIC, CHOPPED
1 TABLESPOON WHITE WINE VINEGAR
GLUG OF OLIVE OIL

Spicy and hearty meals like this are the most satisfying lunches and dinners out there.

- Heat the oil in a large high-sided pan, add the chicken thighs, skin-side down, and fry over medium heat for about 8 minutes or until golden. Turn over the chicken thighs and push to one side of the pan. Add three-quarters of the chopped onions and fry for 5 minutes, or until they start to soften and take on some color. Add the garlic, paprika, chili flakes, cinnamon, and cumin and fry for 1 minute. Tip in the rice, chickpeas, and tomatoes. Put the bouillon (stock) cube into the empty tomato can, top off with boiling water, stir to dissolve, and then add to the pan along with another 2 cans boiling water. Stir well and cook for 30 minutes. If the pan looks like it is drying out, add a splash more water.
- Turn off the heat. Remove the chicken from the pan and rest on a board for 5 minutes, then use two forks to shred the chicken, discarding any skin and bones. Return the meat to the pan.
- Put the remaining onion in a small bowl with the vinegar and sugar, stir to dissolve, and let stand for 2 minutes.
- Put the avocado into a food processor with 2 tablespoons water, the chopped garlic, vinegar, and a glug of olive oil, and process until completely smooth.
- Season the stew with salt and pepper then ladle into bowls and top with the pickled onions and avocado cream.

CAN OF CHOPPED TOMATOES

SHAKSHUKA (BASIC RECIPE)

SERVES 2
PREPARATION TIME: 10 MINUTES
COOKING TIME: 25–30 MINUTES

1 TABLESPOON OLIVE OIL
1 ONION, CHOPPED
2 CLOVES GARLIC, FINELY CHOPPED
1 TEASPOON CHILI FLAKES
1 × 14-OZ/400-G CAN CHOPPED TOMATOES
2 EGGS
SALT AND FRESHLY GROUND BLACK PEPPER

This is a brilliantly versatile Middle Eastern brunch dish that works just as well for breakfast, lunch, or dinner.

- For the tomato sauce, heat the oil in a large skillet (frying pan), add the onion, and cook over medium heat for 5–10 minutes, until softened and translucent. Add the garlic and cook for another 1 minute. Add the chili flakes, tomatoes, and plenty of seasoning, then simmer for 10 minutes, or until the sauce is reduced slightly and thickened.
- Make 2 holes in the tomato sauce, then crack an egg into each hole, and cook for another 5–8 minutes, depending on how you like your egg.

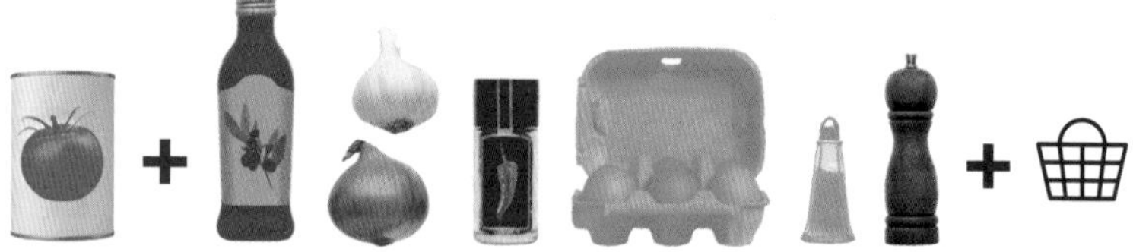

SPICY BEEF AND CILANTRO SHAKSHUKA

FROM THE STORE:
GROUND (MINCED) BEEF
CILANTRO (CORIANDER)

1 × SHAKSHUKA (BASIC RECIPE) INGREDIENTS
7 OZ/200 G GROUND (MINCED) BEEF
1 TEASPOON GROUND CINNAMON
1 TEASPOON CUMIN SEEDS, BASHED
HANDFUL CILANTRO (CORIANDER), LEAVES PICKED

- Follow the basic recipe for shakshuka (above), adding the beef, cinnamon, and cumin with the onion, then continue the recipe as above. Sprinkle with the cilantro (coriander) to finish.

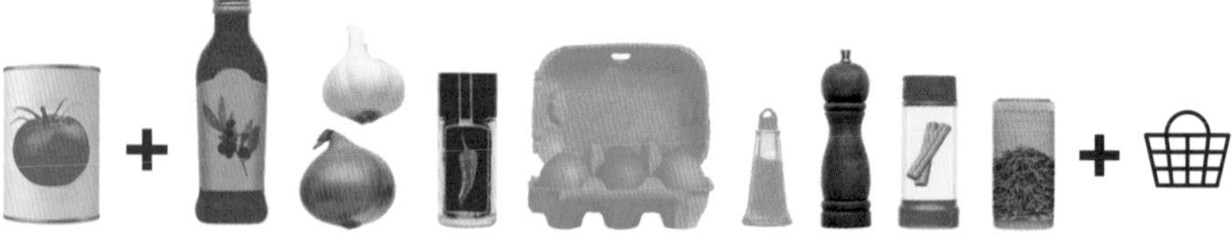

SPINACH AND RICOTTA SHAKSHUKA

FROM THE STORE:
SPINACH
RICOTTA CHEESE

1 × SHAKSHUKA (BASIC RECIPE) INGREDIENTS
3½ OZ/100 G SPINACH
½ CUP (4 OZ/120 G) RICOTTA CHEESE
CHILI FLAKES, FOR SPRINKLING
GLUG OF OLIVE OIL

- Follow the basic recipe for shakshuka (opposite), adding the spinach to the tomato sauce after 8 minutes cooking time, allowing the heat of the sauce to wilt the leaves. Continue the recipe as opposite, then add the ricotta in generous dollops and finish with an extra sprinkle of chili flakes and a glug of olive oil.

 +     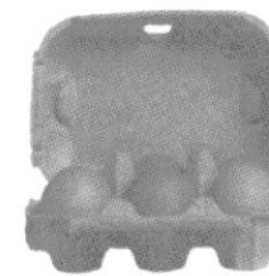  + 

RED BELL PEPPER AND AVOCADO SHAKSHUKA

FROM THE STORE:
RED BELL PEPPER
AVOCADO

1 × SHAKSHUKA (BASIC RECIPE) INGREDIENTS
1 RED BELL PEPPER, THINLY SLICED
1 TEASPOON CUMIN SEEDS, BASHED
1 AVOCADO, PEELED, PITTED, AND DICED, TO SERVE

- Follow the basic recipe for shakshuka (opposite), adding the red bell pepper and cumin with the onion, then continue with the recipe as opposite.
- To serve, arrange the avocado on top of the sauce.

 +     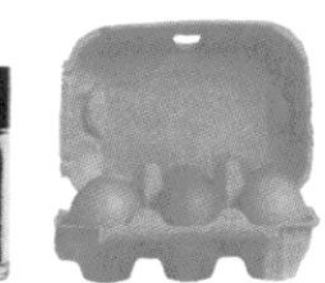   + 

ROASTED SWEET POTATO, CHICKPEA, AND TOMATO STEW WITH GARLIC YOGURT

SERVES 4–6
PREPARATION TIME: 10 MINUTES
COOKING TIME: 30 MINUTES

FROM THE STORE:
SWEET POTATOES
GREEK YOGURT

2 SWEET POTATOES, CUT INTO ¾-INCH/2-CM DICE
3 TABLESPOONS OLIVE OIL
1 ONION, SLICED
2 CLOVES GARLIC, FINELY CHOPPED
2 TEASPOONS CUMIN SEEDS, BASHED
1 TEASPOON GROUND CINNAMON
1 TEASPOON CHILI FLAKES
1 × 14-OZ/400-G CAN CHOPPED TOMATOES
2 TEASPOONS WHITE WINE VINEGAR
1 BOUILLON (STOCK) CUBE
14-OZ/400-G CAN CHICKPEAS, DRAINED AND RINSED
SALT AND FRESHLY GROUND BLACK PEPPER

FOR THE GARLIC YOGURT
1 CUP (8 FL OZ/250 ML) GREEK YOGURT
1 CLOVE GARLIC, CRUSHED
½ TEASPOON SALT
OLIVE OIL, TO DRIZZLE

TIP:
THIS DISH FREEZES REALLY WELL, MINUS THE YOGURT, SO YOU CAN MAKE IT IN ADVANCE.

This vegetarian stew is warming and spicy, and given a little lift with creamy garlic yogurt.

- Preheat the oven to 400°F/200°C/Gas mark 6.
- Put the sweet potato onto 2 baking sheets, drizzle with 1 tablespoon oil, toss to coat, then roast in the hot oven for 20 minutes, turning halfway through, until starting to soften and char at the edges.
- Meanwhile, heat the remaining oil in a large, deep skillet (frying pan), add the onion, and cook gently over medium heat for 10–12 minutes, or until softened. Add the garlic, cook for a minute or two, then add the spices and some salt and pepper, and cook for another 1 minute, or until fragrant. Add the roasted sweet potato, tomatoes, and vinegar.
- Crumble the bouillon (stock) cube into the empty tomato can and fill to the top with boiling water, stir to dissolve, and then pour into the stew. Bring to a simmer and cook for 15 minutes, or until the sauce has thickened and the sweet potatoes are really tender. Add the chickpeas and cook for 2 minutes, or until heated through.
- After you've added the chickpeas, mix the yogurt, garlic, and salt together in a bowl, drizzle with a little oil, then serve with the stew.

ITALIAN MEATBALL AND TOMATO SAUCE SUB

SERVES 4
PREPARATION TIME: 15 MINUTES
COOKING TIME: 30–35 MINUTES

FROM THE STORE:
BAGUETTE OR SUBMARINE ROLLS
GROUND (MINCED) BEEF

1 BAGUETTE OR 4 SUBMARINE ROLLS, SPLIT LENGTHWISE
2–3 TABLESPOONS MILK
1 LB 2 OZ/500 G GROUND (MINCED) BEEF
1 ONION, FINELY CHOPPED
2 CLOVES GARLIC, FINELY CHOPPED
1 TEASPOON OLIVE OIL
SALT AND FRESHLY GROUND BLACK PEPPER
WHOLE GRAIN MUSTARD, TO SERVE (OPTIONAL)

FOR THE TOMATO SAUCE
1 TABLESPOON OLIVE OIL
1 CLOVE GARLIC, CHOPPED
1 TEASPOON DRIED OREGANO
1 TEASPOON DRIED THYME
1 × 14-OZ/400-G CAN CHOPPED TOMATOES
1 TEASPOON SUPERFINE (CASTER) SUGAR
DASH OF WHITE WINE VINEGAR
PINCH OF CHILI FLAKES
SALT AND FRESHLY GROUND BLACK PEPPER

These meatballs with tomato sauce are as good in a submarine-style roll as they are on top of pasta. They freeze well, too—perfect for those wintery nights when cooking dinner seems too much of an effort. Choose a ground (minced) meat with at least 10 percent fat if you can, because it will really boost the flavor.

- To make the meatballs, slice the baguette or rolls in half, then remove some of the inside of the bread, ripping it into small bread crumbs. Put the bread crumbs into a dish with the milk, allowing them to soak it up. Put the beef, onion, and garlic into a large bowl, add the soaked bread, and season generously. Use your hands to combine the mixture, squeezing the meat between your fingers for about 5 minutes. This will help to combine the mixture and prevent the meatballs from falling apart during cooking. Roll the mixture into ping-pong-size balls; you should end up with about 20 meatballs.
- Heat a little oil in a skillet (frying pan), add the meatballs, in 2–3 batches, and fry over medium heat for about 5 minutes, or until browned. Remove from the skillet and set aside on a plate. Add more oil if the meatballs begin to stick.
- To make the sauce, heat the oil in a large skillet. Add the garlic and cook for 1 minute, then add the dried herbs, tomatoes, seasoning, sugar, vinegar, and chili flakes. Taste to check the flavor, adding more salt, sugar, or vinegar if you need to, then bring to a boil, reduce the heat, and simmer for 5 minutes. Add the meatballs and simmer for another 10–15 minutes until the meatballs are cooked through. If the sauce is becoming too thick, add a splash of water and oil—the sauce should coat the meatballs.
- To serve, pile the saucy meatballs into the fresh baguette or sub rolls and serve with some mustard if you like.

TOMATO AND CHORIZO STEW

SERVES 4
PREPARATION TIME: 10 MINUTES
COOKING TIME: 25 MINUTES

FROM THE STORE:
CHORIZO SAUSAGE
FLAT-LEAF PARSLEY

1 TABLESPOON OLIVE OIL
1 ONION, THINLY SLICED
7 OZ/200 G CHORIZO SAUSAGE, SLICED
2 CLOVES GARLIC, CHOPPED
1 TABLESPOON SMOKED PAPRIKA
½ TEASPOON DRIED THYME
½ TEASPOON CHILI FLAKES
1 × 14-OZ/400-G CAN CHOPPED TOMATOES
1 BOUILLON (STOCK) CUBE
1 × 14-OZ/400-G CAN CHICKPEAS, DRAINED AND RINSED
1 TEASPOON SUPERFINE (CASTER) SUGAR
1 TEASPOON WHITE WINE VINEGAR
HANDFUL FLAT-LEAF PARSLEY, COARSELY CHOPPED
SALT AND FRESHLY GROUND BLACK PEPPER

TIP:
IF YOU WANT TO INCREASE YOUR VEGETABLE INTAKE, REPLACE THE FLAT-LEAF PARSLEY WITH A 3-OZ/80-G BAG OF BABY LEAF SPINACH OR WATERCRESS AND STIR IT INTO THE STEW AT THE END OF COOKING. THE HEAT OF THE STEW WILL WILT THE LEAVES.

Spanish flavors add sunshine to your day at any time of the year. Instead of sprinkling with parsley, try adding some whole uncooked shrimp (prawns) at the end of cooking to turn this dish into surf 'n' turf.

- Heat the oil in a Dutch oven (casserole dish) or large high-sided skillet (frying pan), add the onion and chorizo, and cook over medium-high heat, stirring frequently, for 5 minutes, or until the onion has softened and the chorizo has released its red oil into the Dutch oven or skillet. Add the garlic, paprika, thyme, and chili flakes and fry for 1 minute, then add the tomatoes.
- Crumble the bouillon (stock) cube into the empty tomato can and fill to the halfway level with boiling water, swirl the can, and then pour the hot broth (stock) into the stew. Bring the mixture to a boil, add the chickpeas, and cook for 15 minutes, or until the stew is rich and slightly reduced. Add the sugar and vinegar with plenty of salt and pepper, then remove from the heat and leave for a few minutes before stirring in the parsley.
- Ladle into bowls and serve.

CREAM OF TOMATO SOUP WITH CHEESE TOASTIES

SERVES 2
PREPARATION TIME: 5 MINUTES
COOKING TIME: 20 MINUTES

FROM THE STORE:
STRONG CHEDDAR CHEESE
CRUSTY LOAF OF BREAD

FOR THE SOUP
1 TABLESPOON OLIVE OIL
1 ONION, CHOPPED
1 CLOVE GARLIC, CHOPPED
1 TEASPOON DRIED OREGANO
¼ TEASPOON CHILI FLAKES
1 × 14-OZ/400-G CAN CHOPPED TOMATOES
½ BOUILLON (STOCK) CUBE
½ TEASPOON SUPERFINE (CASTER) SUGAR
1 CUP (8 FL OZ/250 ML) MILK
SALT AND FRESHLY GROUND BLACK PEPPER

FOR THE TOASTIES
GENEROUS ¾ CUP (3½ OZ/100 G) GRATED STRONG CHEDDAR CHEESE
2 TEASPOONS WHOLE GRAIN MUSTARD
SPLASH OF MILK
4 THICK SLICES BREAD FROM A CRUSTY LOAF

TIP:
THERE'S NO NEED TO THROW LEFTOVER BREAD AWAY, PROCESS IT INTO BREAD CRUMBS AND FREEZE FOR UP TO 2 MONTHS. THESE BREAD CRUMBS MAKE THE PERFECT CRISPY TOPPING FOR MAC 'N' CHEESE (SEE PAGE 138).

Cream of tomato soup is just about the most delicious, warming, and comforting food available. Our version is lighter as we use milk to make the soup creamy rather than heavy (double) cream. The perfect partner to this sumptuous soup is a cheese toastie. Or, try it with a Zucchini and Basil Muffin (see page 131).

- Heat the oil in a large pan, add the onion, and cook over medium heat for 5 minutes, or until starting to soften and turn golden. Add the garlic, oregano, and chili flakes and cook for another 1 minute. Add the tomatoes then crumble the bouillon (stock) cube and sugar into the empty tomato can. Fill the can with ⅔ cup (5 fl oz/150 ml) boiling water, stir to dissolve the bouillon cube, then pour this into the soup pan. Bring to a boil, reduce the heat, and simmer for 10 minutes. Pour in the milk and add plenty of seasoning.
- Remove the soup from the heat and, using a handheld blender, blend until smooth—you don't have to do this but it will be reminiscent of a store-bought favorite if you do! Set the soup over low heat to keep warm while you make your toasties.
- Heat the broiler (grill) to medium-high. Stir the cheese, mustard, and milk together in a large bowl. Lay 2 slices of bread on a baking sheet, spread each slice generously with the cheese mixture, and sandwich with the remaining bread. Cook under the broiler for 1–2 minutes until golden brown, then carefully flip over and broil (grill) the other side—the cheese should be bubbling and melted and the bread crisp and golden.
- Ladle the soup into mugs or bowls and serve with the molten cheese toasties.

CHICKEN THIGHS WITH GREEN BEANS IN SPICED TOMATO SAUCE

SERVES 2
PREPARATION TIME: 10 MINUTES, PLUS 5 MINUTES STANDING
COOKING TIME: 25 MINUTES

FROM THE STORE:
CHICKEN THIGHS
STRING (RUNNER) BEANS

4 CHICKEN THIGHS, ON THE BONE AND SKIN STILL ON
2 TABLESPOONS OLIVE OIL, PLUS EXTRA FOR DRIZZLING
1 TEASPOON SMOKED PAPRIKA
½ TEASPOON DRIED THYME
½ TEASPOON DRIED OREGANO
SALT AND FRESHLY GROUND BLACK PEPPER

FOR THE GREEN BEANS
1 ONION, FINELY SLICED
2 CLOVES GARLIC, SLICED
1 × 14-OZ/400-G CAN CHOPPED TOMATOES
½ TEASPOON GROUND CINNAMON
½ TEASPOON SMOKED PAPRIKA
½ TEASPOON CHILI FLAKES
7 OZ/200 G STRING (RUNNER) BEANS, SLICED

TIP:
LEAVE ANY LEFTOVER BEANS IN THE TOMATO SAUCE TO COOL AND SERVE THE DISH AS PART OF A MEZZE LUNCH WITH FLATBREADS AND GARLIC YOGURT (SEE PAGE 70).

Cooking the green beans in spiced tomato sauce brings a new, exciting flavor to a vegetable that is often just boiled and left to linger on your plate alongside its more popuar and interesting vegetable relatives. If you can't find string (runner) beans swap them for any other green bean.

- Put the chicken thighs on a plate, drizzle with oil, sprinkle with the paprika, dried herbs, and plenty of seasoning, and leave for 5 minutes.
- Put a large nonstick skillet (frying pan) over medium heat. When hot, add the chicken thighs, skin-side down, and cook for 10 minutes until the skin is golden and crisp, and most of the fat has been rendered from the skin. Turn over and continue cooking for 5 minutes, or until the chicken thighs are cooked through. Remove from the skillet, cover, and keep warm.
- Tip out all but a coating of fat from the skillet. Add the onion and garlic and cook for 2 minutes. Add the tomatoes, cinnamon, paprika, and chili flakes and let boil for 2 minutes. Add the string (runner) beans and continue to cook for about 5 minutes, until the sauce has thickened and the beans are just tender. Remove from the heat, season with plenty of salt and pepper, and serve with the crisp chicken thighs.

SHRIMP AND TOMATO CURRY

SERVES 2
PREPARATION TIME: 5 MINUTES
COOKING TIME: 20–25 MINUTES

FROM THE STORE:
BABY LEAF SPINACH
JUMBO SHRIMP (KING PRAWNS)

1 TEASPOON CUMIN SEEDS
1 TEASPOON MUSTARD SEEDS
1 TEASPOON CHILI FLAKES
1 TABLESPOON OLIVE OIL
1 ONION, SLICED
2 CLOVES GARLIC, CHOPPED
2 TEASPOONS GROUND TURMERIC
1 × 14-OZ/400-G CAN CHOPPED TOMATOES
1 TABLESPOON WHITE WINE VINEGAR
½ TEASPOON SUPERFINE (CASTER) SUGAR
3½-OZ/100-G BAG BABY LEAF SPINACH
7 OZ/200-G COOKED JUMBO SHRIMP (KING PRAWNS)
SALT AND FRESHLY GROUND BLACK PEPPER
FRESHLY COOKED WHITE BASMATI RICE, TO SERVE

TIP:
YOU CAN FREEZE THE CURRY BASE, THEN DEFROST IT AND ADD THE SHRIMP (PRAWNS) WHEN YOU ARE HEATING IT THROUGH. COOK UNTIL PIPING HOT.

You don't have to use shrimp (prawns) in this curry; paneer (Indian cheese), shredded leftover chicken, or even a trusty can of chickpeas would work well here.

- Dry-fry the cumin and mustard seeds in a large nonstick skillet (frying pan) for 2 minutes, or until the seeds start to pop and smell fragrant. Put them into a mortar and, using the pestle, bash to a rough powder with the chili flakes—you can use a bowl and the end of a rolling pin or flat jar if you don't have a mortar and pestle.
- Put the skillet back over the heat and pour in the oil. When it is hot, add the onion and cook for 5 minutes, or until starting to soften. Add the garlic, toasted spices, and turmeric and fry for 1 minute. Add the tomatoes, vinegar, and sugar and cook for about 10 minutes, or until the sauce has thickened. Season with salt and pepper then stir in the spinach, allowing the heat of the skillet to wilt the leaves. Stir in the shrimp (prawns) and cook for 3–5 minutes or until piping hot. Serve the curry with cooked white rice.

SPICY TOMATO GRANITA

SERVES 4–6
PREPARATION TIME: 5 MINUTES, PLUS UP TO 4 HOURS FREEZING TIME

FROM THE STORE:
LEMON
TABASCO SAUCE

1 × 14-OZ/400-G CAN CHOPPED TOMATOES
ZEST AND JUICE OF 1 LEMON
TABASCO SAUCE, TO TASTE, PLUS EXTRA TO SERVE
DASH OF SOY SAUCE
SALT AND FRESHLY GROUND BLACK PEPPER

We've had this as a hangover cure, a palate cleanser after a big meal, and a refreshing treat on a summer's day.

- Put all the ingredients into a food processor, pour in ⅔ cup (5 fl oz/150 ml) water, and blend to a puree. Spoon the puree into a plastic freezerproof container and freeze for 30 minutes. Remove from the freezer, then scrape the granita with a fork to break up the ice crystals. Repeat this every 60 minutes until the granita is frozen and broken into lots of tiny flakes.
- To serve, spoon into glasses and add a few more dashes of Tabasco.

BAG OF FLOUR

TURKISH PIDE (BASIC RECIPE)

MAKES 4
PREPARATION TIME: 20 MINUTES, PLUS 5 MINUTES RESTING
COOKING TIME: 15 MINUTES

- 3⅓ CUPS (14 OZ/400 G) ALL-PURPOSE (PLAIN) FLOUR, PLUS EXTRA FOR DUSTING
- 1 TEASPOON SALT
- 1 TEASPOON SUPERFINE (CASTER) SUGAR
- 4 TABLESPOONS OLIVE OIL, PLUS EXTRA FOR BRUSHING

This is a quick and simple flatbread that you can adapt with all manner of toppings; here are some of our favorites, but we also love halloumi and za'atar spice mix, or just a simple garlic butter with cilantro (coriander) as a side dish to a stew.

- To make the pide dough, mix the flour, salt, and sugar in a large bowl, then make a well in the middle. Gradually add the oil and about 1 cup (8 fl oz/250 ml) water or enough to bring all the ingredients together to form a soft, smooth dough. You might need up to 2 tablespoons more water, though. Knead the dough for 5–8 minutes. Let rest for 5 minutes, then divide into 4 pieces.
- Preheat the oven to 400°F/200°C/Gas mark 6 and line a baking sheet with parchment (baking) paper.
- Lightly flour a work counter and roll out each piece of dough into a long oval shape. Transfer to the prepared baking sheet and fill with your chosen toppings, leaving a ¾ inch/2 cm border around the edges. Twist both ends of the dough and push the border in and up a little to enclose the filling. Bake in the hot oven for 12–15 minutes, or until golden. Brush the dough with a little olive oil before serving.

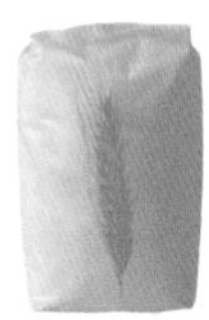 +    +

ROASTED RED PEPPER AND FETA PIDE

FROM THE STORE:
ROASTED RED BELL PEPPERS
FETA CHEESE

- 1 × TURKISH PIDE (BASIC RECIPE) INGREDIENTS
- 3 ROASTED RED BELL PEPPERS FROM A JAR, THINLY SLICED
- 1½ CUPS (7 OZ/200 G) CRUMBLED FETA CHEESE
- PINCH OF CHILI FLAKES

- Make the pide dough as in the basic recipe, above, then divide the bell peppers, feta, and chili flakes among the 4 pide and bake as above.

 +   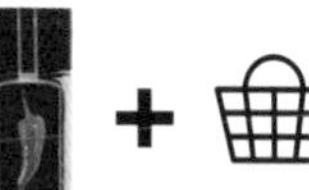

BEEF AND CHILE PIDE

FROM THE STORE:
GROUND (MINCED) BEEF
GREEN CHILES

1 × TURKISH PIDE (BASIC RECIPE) INGREDIENTS
7 OZ/200 G GROUND (MINCED) BEEF
1 TEASPOON GROUND CINNAMON
2 TEASPOONS SMOKED PAPRIKA
2 GREEN CHILES, CHOPPED

- Make the pide dough as in the basic recipe, opposite. Mix the beef, spices, and chiles together in a bowl, then divide among the 4 pide and bake as opposite.

 +  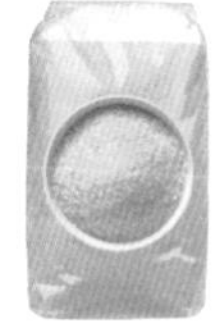   

PEPPERONI, CHEESE, AND EGG PIDE

FROM THE STORE:
PEPPERONI
STRONG CHEDDAR CHEESE

1 × TURKISH PIDE (BASIC RECIPE) INGREDIENTS
16 SLICES PEPPERONI
GENEROUS ¾ CUP (3½ OZ/100 G) GRATED STRONG CHEDDAR CHEESE
4 EGGS

- Make the pide as in the basic recipe, opposite, then divide the pepperoni and grated cheese among the pide. Crack an egg on top of each pide and bake as above.

 +   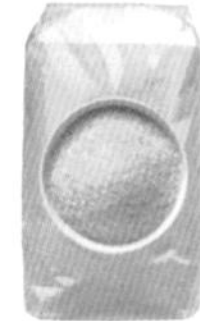  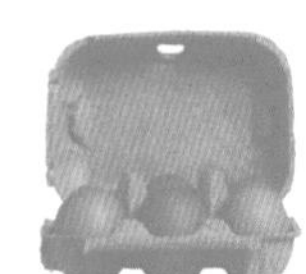 

SHRIMP AND SCALLION DIM SUM WITH SOY DIPPING SAUCE

SERVES 4–6
PREPARATION TIME: 25 MINUTES
COOKING TIME: 5 MINUTES

FROM THE STORE:
UNCOOKED SHRIMP (PRAWNS)
SCALLIONS (SPRING ONIONS)

FOR THE WRAPPERS
1 EGG
LARGE PINCH OF SALT
1¼ CUPS (5 OZ/150 G) ALL-PURPOSE (PLAIN) FLOUR, PLUS EXTRA FOR DUSTING

FOR THE FILLING
9 OZ/250 G UNCOOKED SHRIMP (PRAWNS), FINELY CHOPPED
3 SCALLIONS (SPRING ONIONS), GREENS AND WHITES FINELY SLICED
1 SMALL CLOVE GARLIC, CRUSHED
1 TEASPOON SOY SAUCE
1 TEASPOON WHITE WINE VINEGAR
1 TEASPOON SUPERFINE (CASTER) SUGAR

FOR THE DIPPING SAUCE
¼ CUP (2 FL OZ/60 ML) SOY SAUCE
1 TEASPOON CHILI FLAKES
2 TEASPOONS SUPERFINE (CASTER) SUGAR
2 SCALLIONS (SPRING ONIONS), VERY FINELY CHOPPED

TIP:
THIS ALSO WORKS WELL WITH GROUND (MINCED) PORK INSTEAD OF THE SHRIMP (PRAWNS), YOU JUST NEED TO REPLACE OUNCE FOR OUNCE AND STEAM UNTIL COOKED THROUGH.

These Asian-inspired packages (parcels) are actually much simpler to make than you'd think. If you make the wrappers in advance, you can freeze the rolled out wrappers in between layers of parchment (baking) paper, then it's just a matter of pulling them out of the freezer 20 minutes before you want to cook.

- To make the wrappers, mix the egg with the salt in a small bowl, then put the flour into a large bowl. Pour in the egg mixture and add just enough water, about ¼ cup (2 fl oz/60 ml), to form a dough. Knead the dough for at least 5–10 minutes on a floured work counter, or until the dough is smooth and soft, then divide into about 20 small balls. Cover the balls with a damp dish towel to stop them drying out while you make the filling and assemble the dim sum.
- Mix all the filling ingredients together in a bowl and lightly flour a baking sheet.
- On a lightly floured work counter, roll a dough ball into a circle, about 4¾ inches/12 cm in diameter, and as thinly as possible—about ⅛ inch/1 mm—but leaving the center slightly thicker to support the filling and avoid tearing. Place 2 teaspoons of the filling in the middle of the dough circle, then either fold the dough over into a crescent shape and pinch the sides together, or draw up the dough around the filling so it looks like a little pouch, then pinch and twist the edges together to secure. Place on the prepared baking sheet and repeat with the rest of the filling and dough balls.
- At this stage, the dim sum can be covered loosely with plastic wrap (clingfilm) and chilled in the refrigerator for a few hours until you are ready to cook, or you can go straight ahead. To cook, cut out small squares of parchment (baking) paper and sit each dumpling on a square of paper. Place the dumplings and paper in a bamboo or metal steamer set over a pan of simmering water, and cook for 5 minutes, or until the shrimp (prawns) are pink and the dough is translucent.
- In a small bowl, mix the dipping sauce ingredients together and serve with the dim sum.

MINI PECAN PIES

MAKES 12
PREPARATION TIME: 15 MINUTES, PLUS 20 MINUTES CHILLING
COOKING TIME: 12–15 MINUTES, PLUS COOLING

FROM THE STORE:

BUTTER
PECANS

FOR THE PIE DOUGH (PASTRY)

- 1½ CUPS (6 OZ/175 G) ALL-PURPOSE (PLAIN) FLOUR, PLUS EXTRA FOR DUSTING
- ½ TEASPOON SALT
- 7 TABLESPOONS (3½ OZ/100 G) BUTTER, DICED
- 1 EGG YOLK

FOR THE FILLING

- 4 TABLESPOONS (2 OZ/50 G) BUTTER, MELTED AND COOLED
- ½ CUP (3½ OZ/100 G) SUPERFINE (CASTER) SUGAR
- 1 EGG
- ½ TEASPOON GROUND CINNAMON
- GENEROUS ½ CUP (3 OZ/80 G) PECANS, CHOPPED

TIP:
TRY ADDING WALNUTS, RAISINS, FINELY CHOPPED DATES, OR EVEN CRANBERRIES INSTEAD OF THE PECANS.

Any North American will know these treats well. Sticky and sickly sweet, they're perfect with a cup of strong black coffee.

- To make the pie dough (pastry), mix the flour and salt together in a large bowl, add the butter, and rub it into the mixture with your fingertips until it resembles fine bread crumbs; this should take about 5 minutes. Make a well in the center of the mixture. Add the egg yolk and 1–2 tablespoons ice-cold water, then mix to form a firm, smooth dough. Wrap the dough in plastic wrap (clingfilm) and chill in the refrigerator for 10 minutes to allow the dough to rest.
- Preheat the oven to 350°F/180°C/Gas mark 4.
- Once the dough has chilled, roll it out on a lightly floured work counter to about ¼ inch/5 mm thick and stamp out 3 inch/8 cm circles to fit a 12-section muffin pan. Chill again in the refrigerator while you make the filling.
- To make the filling, mix all the ingredients together in a bowl.
- Remove the muffin pan from the refrigerator and fill each muffin section with an equal amount of the pecan filling and leave a little room for the filling to rise during cooking. Bake for 12–15 minutes, or until the filling is set and golden. Cool in the pan for 10 minutes, then cool completely on a wire rack.

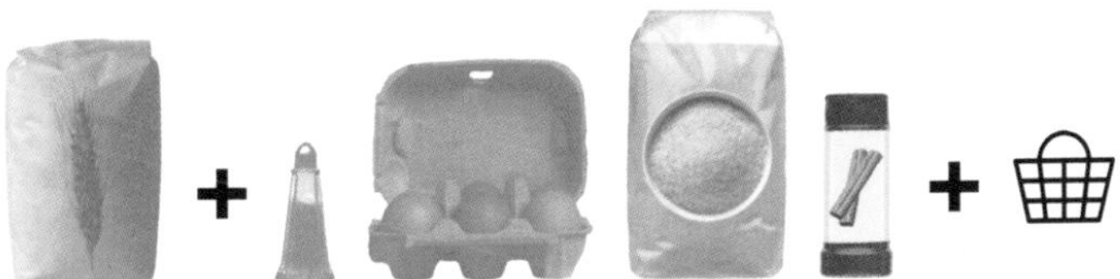

SQUASH DUMPLINGS

SERVES 4
PREPARATION TIME: 15 MINUTES
COOKING TIME: 30 MINUTES

FROM THE STORE:
BUTTERNUT SQUASH
ITALIAN PARMESAN CHEESE

1 LARGE BUTTERNUT SQUASH, PEELED, SEEDED, AND CUBED (YOU WILL NEED ABOUT 1¾ LB/800 G)
1½ CUPS (6 OZ/175 G) ALL-PURPOSE (PLAIN) FLOUR
1 EGG
5 TABLESPOONS OLIVE OIL, PLUS EXTRA FOR OILING
2 CLOVES GARLIC, THINLY SLICED
½ TEASPOON CHILI FLAKES (OPTIONAL)
SALT AND FRESHLY GROUND BLACK PEPPER
1 CUP (2¾ OZ/75 G) FINELY GRATED ITALIAN PARMESAN CHEESE, TO SERVE

TIP:
IF YOU DO NOT HAVE SQUASH THEN SUBSTITUTE IT FOR POTATOES—YOU WILL MAKE PERFECT GNOCCHI. JUST MAKE SURE YOU GET YOUR POTATOES REALLY DRY BEFORE ADDING THE FLOUR SO YOUR DUMPLINGS ARE NOT GLUEY.

This is our version of Claudia Roden's pumpkin gnocchetti—it is insanely good. It is a cross between German spätzle and traditional Italian gnocchi. The dumpling dough resembles a thick batter more than a stiff dough, so don't be alarmed, we promise it will work! We have included it because it epitomizes really simple cooking with very limited ingredients.

- Put the squash into a large pan and pour in enough water to cover. Bring to a boil, then reduce the heat and simmer for 15 minutes, or until the squash is very tender. Drain well, then return to the pan, set over low heat, and let the squash completely dry—keep it moving to drive off any cooking water. This will take about 3 minutes. When you are satisfied that most of the water has dried up, mash the squash with a potato masher and beat again to remove any remaining water.
- Season the squash generously with salt and pepper, then beat in the flour and egg until fully combined.
- Lightly oil a baking sheet and set aside. Bring a large pan of water to a boil, then add some salt. Oil 2 tablespoons, then use one spoon to scoop up heaping tablespoons of the mixture, and use the other spoon to push the mixture off into the boiling water. The dumplings will float to the top of the water. Cook them for 2 minutes, then remove with a slotted spoon and drain by laying them on the prepared baking sheet while you continue to cook the remaining dumplings.
- Once all the dumplings are cooked, heat 5 tablespoons oil in a skillet (frying pan) over medium heat. Add the garlic and sizzle for 1–2 minutes until light golden, then throw in the chili flakes, if using. Divide the dumplings among warmed plates and spoon over the oil and garlic slithers. Serve with a generous amount of grated Parmesan.

SMOKY GARLIC MONKEY BUBBLE BREAD

SERVES 10
PREPARATION TIME: 45 MINUTES, PLUS 1¾ HOURS RISING
COOKING TIME: 35–40 MINUTES

FROM THE STORE:
BUTTER
ACTIVE DRY (FAST-ACTION) YEAST

5 TABLESPOONS (2¾ OZ/75 G) BUTTER, PLUS EXTRA FOR GREASING
1 CUP (8 FL OZ/250 ML) MILK
SCANT 4¼ CUPS (1 LB 2 OZ/500 G) ALL-PURPOSE (PLAIN) FLOUR, PLUS EXTRA FOR DUSTING
1 × ¼-OZ/7-G SACHET ACTIVE DRY (FAST-ACTION) YEAST
1 TEASPOON SUPERFINE (CASTER) SUGAR
1 TEASPOON SALT
1 EGG
OLIVE OIL, FOR OILING AND DRIZZLING

FOR THE COATING
1¼ STICKS (5 OZ/150 G) BUTTER, MELTED
2 CLOVES GARLIC, FINELY CHOPPED
2 TEASPOONS SMOKED PAPRIKA

This savory take on the normally sugar and cinnamon-packed monkey bubble bread is the perfect accompaniment to curries, soups, and stews, or for a few casual drinks. If you don't have a bundt pan, use an 8½–10-inch/22–25-cm deep cake pan instead. The beauty of this recipe is the ability to prepare ahead; once dipped in the garlic butter, you can chill it in the refrigerator for up to 8 hours, or overnight, or even wrap tightly in plastic wrap (clingfilm) and then a layer of aluminum foil and freeze for up to a month, then return to room temperature and cook.

- Lightly grease a 15-cup (120-fl oz/3½-liter) bundt or cake pan with butter.
- Put the butter and milk into a small pan and warm over low heat for 2–3 minutes to just above room temperature until the butter has melted, then remove from the heat and cool to lukewarm.
- Mix the flour, yeast, sugar, and salt together in a large bowl. Whisk the egg into the milk mixture, then stir into the flour. Mix until it forms a dough. Knead on a floured work counter for about 10 minutes, or until the dough is smooth and elastic. Put the dough in a clean, oiled bowl, cover with plastic wrap (clingfilm), and let rise in a warm place for 1 hour, or until doubled in size.
- Line a baking sheet with parchment (baking) paper. Cut the dough in half, then pinch each half into about 25 pieces. Roll each piece into a small ball, about the size of a ping-pong ball, and put on the parchment paper, covering with a dish towel as you go, to prevent them drying out.
- Put the melted butter into a small bowl with the garlic and paprika. Dip 1 ball into the butter and put in the prepared pan. Repeat with the other balls, until they are evenly spread across the whole pan. Drizzle with any remaining butter. At this point, you can chill the dough in the refrigerator for a few hours or overnight, or continue to cook.
- Whether chilled or not, cover the bundt pan in plastic wrap and let rise again for 30–45 minutes until the balls have puffed up.
- Meanwhile, preheat the oven to 350°F/180°C/Gas mark 4.
- Once the balls have risen, bake in the oven for 30–35 minutes, or until the butter is bubbling at the sides and the dough is golden. Cool in the pan for 5 minutes, then put a plate over the top, tip upside down to loosen, and serve.

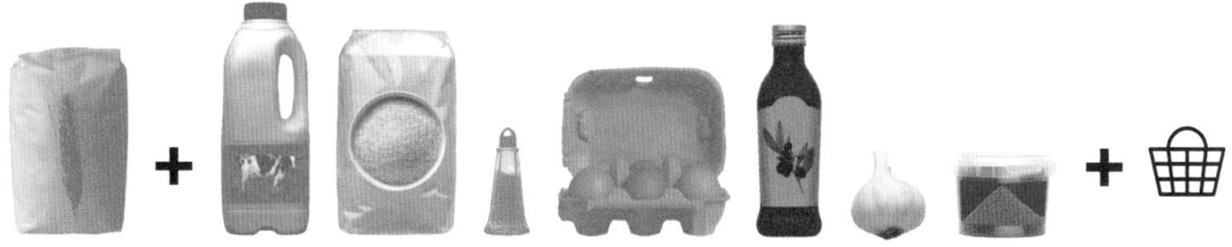

SKILLET PIZZA

SERVES 4
PREPARATION TIME: 20 MINUTES, PLUS 1 HOUR RISING
COOKING TIME: 30–40 MINUTES

FROM THE STORE:
ACTIVE DRY (FAST-ACTION) YEAST
MOZZARELLA CHEESE

- 3⅓ CUPS (14 OZ/400 G) ALL-PURPOSE (PLAIN) FLOUR, PLUS EXTRA FOR DUSTING
- 1 TABLESPOON SUPERFINE (CASTER) SUGAR
- 1 TEASPOON SALT
- 1 × ¼-OZ/7-G SACHET ACTIVE DRY (FAST-ACTION) YEAST
- 2 TABLESPOONS OLIVE OIL, PLUS EXTRA FOR OILING AND DRIZZLING

FOR THE TOPPING

- ½ × 14-OZ/400-G CAN CHOPPED TOMATOES
- 1 CLOVE GARLIC, CHOPPED
- ½ TEASPOON CHILI FLAKES, PLUS EXTRA TO SERVE
- 9 OZ/250 G MOZZARELLA CHEESE, PATTED DRY ON PAPER TOWELS AND TORN
- SALT AND FRESHLY GROUND BLACK PEPPER

TIP:
YOU CAN COOK YOUR PIZZA BASES IN THE SKILLET (FRYING PAN) FOR 3 MINUTES WITHOUT THE TOPPING THEN FLASH UNDER THE HOT BROILER (GRILL) FOR 1 MINUTE TO "SET" THE SURFACE. THE BASES CAN THEN BE COOLED AND TOPPED LATER—SIMPLY FINISH IN A HOT OVEN, 400°F/200°C/GAS MARK 6, FOR 10 MINUTES.

This recipe is to get you started on making delicious pizza at home. It is such a simple and effective method with perfect results every time—the skillet (frying pan) and broiler (grill) combo ensure that your pizza comes into contact with the high heat required to give a crisp, yet pillowy bottom. You have to try it to believe it—we've kept it simple with a pizza Margherita but experiment with your favorite toppings.

- Mix the flour, sugar, salt, and yeast together in a large bowl until well combined. Make a well in the center of the flour mixture and pour in the oil followed by about 1 cup (8 fl oz/250 ml) warm (but not hot) water. Bring together to form a soft dough—it should not be really sticky or very dry. Add a little more flour or a drop more water as necessary. Tip the dough out onto a lightly floured work counter and knead for 10 minutes, or until smooth and elastic. Put the dough into a lightly oiled bowl, cover with plastic wrap (clingfilm), and let rise in a warm place for about 1 hour, or until doubled in size.
- Meanwhile, in a bowl, mix the tomatoes with the garlic, chili flakes, and plenty of salt and pepper. Set aside.
- Once the dough has doubled in size, punch the surface down with your fist to remove any air. Tip it out onto a lightly floured work counter and knead for 2 minutes. Divide the dough into 4 equal portions.
- Heat the broiler (grill) to high. Using a rolling pin or lightly oiled hands, flatten out 1 piece of dough into a 10 inch/25 cm circle. At this point put a large ovenproof nonstick skillet (frying pan) over high heat. When the skillet is really hot (nearly smoking) carefully put your pizza base into the skillet and cook for 2½–3 minutes. This will seal the pizza base and form a crisp crust. Place the pizza under the hot broiler for 1 minute. If it puffs up, press it down. Remove from the oven.
- Spoon a quarter of the tomato sauce over the surface of the pizza base leaving a ½ inch/1 cm border. Sprinkle over a quarter of the mozzarella cheese, then cook under the hot broiler for 3 minutes, or until the crust bubbles and chars lightly at the edges and the mozzarella is molten. Slide the pizza onto a baking sheet and keep warm while you continue cooking your pizzas. Alternatively, cut the pizza into wedges and eat immediately before cooking the next one.

CHILI CHOCOLATE PROFITEROLES

SERVES 4
PREPARATION TIME: 15 MINUTES
COOKING TIME: 30 MINUTES, PLUS COOLING

FROM THE STORE:
BUTTER
HEAVY (DOUBLE) CREAM

6 TABLESPOONS (3 OZ/85 G) COLD BUTTER, DICED
SCANT 1¼ CUPS (5 OZ/140 G) ALL-PURPOSE (PLAIN) FLOUR, SIFTED
3 EGGS, LIGHTLY BEATEN

FOR THE TOPPING
7 OZ/200 G BITTERSWEET (DARK) CHOCOLATE, COARSELY CHOPPED
½ TEASPOON CHILI FLAKES, PLUS EXTRA FOR SPRINKLING

FOR THE FILLING
2½ CUPS (20 FL OZ/600 ML) HEAVY (DOUBLE) CREAM
3 TABLESPOONS SUPERFINE (CASTER) SUGAR

TIP:
UNFILLED BAKED PROFITEROLES FREEZE REALLY WELL (FOR UP TO A MONTH), MAKING THEM THE PERFECT DESSERT TO WHIP OUT WHEN YOU WANT TO IMPRESS BUT ARE SHORT ON TIME. SIMPLY CRISP IN A HOT OVEN, COOL THEN FILL WITH CREAM.

It's unlikely that you will be making these every day but once you master choux pastry you will realize how easy and versatile it can be. Deep fry it in oil and roll in superfine (caster) sugar and you have churros or pipe into fingers or rings and fill with whipped cream for eclairs or Paris Brest...the list goes on.

- Preheat the oven to 400°F/200°C/Gas mark 6.
- Put the butter into a medium pan with scant 1 cup (7¾ fl oz/225 ml) water and heat gently over low heat for 5 minutes until the butter is melted. Increase the heat and bring the mixture to a boil, then remove the pan from the heat, add the flour, and beat with a wooden spoon until you have a smooth, shiny dough that leaves the sides of the pan. Tip into a large bowl and cool for 5 minutes.
- Gradually add the eggs to the mixture, beating with a wooden spoon after each addition until all of the egg is added and you have a smooth dough that falls reluctantly from the spoon.
- Line a couple of baking sheets with parchment (baking) paper, then use 2 tablespoons to dollop heaping tablespoon-size balls, about 2 inches/5 cm in diameter, onto the paper, leaving about ¾ inch/2 cm between each ball. Smooth any peaks in the dough with a damp finger and bake in the hot oven for 20–25 minutes, or until puffed, golden, and crisp. Remove from the oven and use the end of a teaspoon to poke a hole into each profiterole.
- Put the profiteroles hole-side up on the prepred baking sheets and return to the oven for 5 minutes to let the profiteroles dry out and crisp up a little more. Remove from the oven and transfer to a wire rack to cool completely.
- To make the topping, put the chocolate into a microwavable bowl with the chili flakes and 3 tablespoons water, and microwave in 20-second intervals, stirring after each one, until the mixture is smooth. Alternatively, put the chocolate, chili flakes, and water into a heatproof bowl set over a pan of gently simmering water, making sure that the bottom of the bowl doesn't touch the water, and leave until melted, then remove from the heat and stir until smooth. Set aside.
- To make the filling, lightly whip the cream and sugar in a large bowl to soft peaks, then spoon into a pastry (piping) bag fitted with an ½ inch/1 cm tip (nozzle) if you have one. If you don't have one, spoon the cream into a sandwich bag and snip off the corner with a pair of scissors. Pipe the cream into the profiteroles. Alternatively, use a spoon to fill the buns with the cream.
- Divide the profiteroles among plates, then spoon over the chocolate sauce and sprinkle with a pinch of extra chili flakes, if you like.

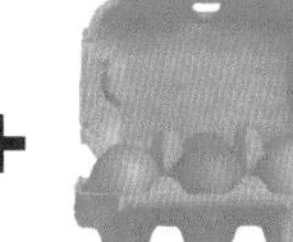

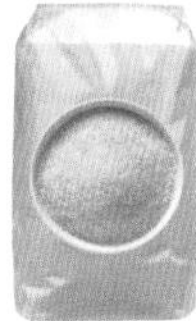

BLUEBERRY AND CINNAMON CLAFOUTIS

SERVES 4
PREPARATION TIME: 10 MINUTES
COOKING TIME: 40 MINUTES

FROM THE STORE:
BUTTER
BLUEBERRIES

2 TABLESPOONS (1 OZ/25 G) BUTTER
GENEROUS ⅓ CUP (2¾ OZ/75 G) SUPERFINE (CASTER) SUGAR
3 CUPS (1 LB/450 G) BLUEBERRIES
3 EGGS
GENEROUS ¾ CUP (3½ OZ/100 G) ALL-PURPOSE (PLAIN) FLOUR
½ TEASPOON BAKING POWDER
½ TEASPOON GROUND CINNAMON
SMALL PINCH OF SALT
½ CUP (4 FL OZ/125 ML) MILK

This classic French dessert is given an all-American spin by using blueberries and cinnamon instead of cherries, but you can use any seasonal fruit you like. Serve warm with a scoop of good-quality vanilla ice cream, if you have any in the freezer.

- Preheat the oven to 350°F/180°C/Gas mark 4.
- Cut off a small amount of the butter and use it to grease a medium ovenproof dish. Sprinkle 1 tablespoon of the sugar over the dish, covering the bottom and sides. Put the blueberries into the prepared dish—they should sit in one layer at the bottom.
- Put the remaining butter into a small pan and melt over low heat, then set aside.
- Put the eggs and remaining sugar into a large bowl and, using an electric whisk, beat together until pale and creamy.
- In another bowl, sift together the flour, baking powder, cinnamon, and salt, then fold into the egg and sugar mixture.
- Mix the melted butter into the milk, then stir into the batter.
- Pour the batter over the fruit and bake in the hot oven for about 30 minutes, or until golden and puffed up. Serve warm.

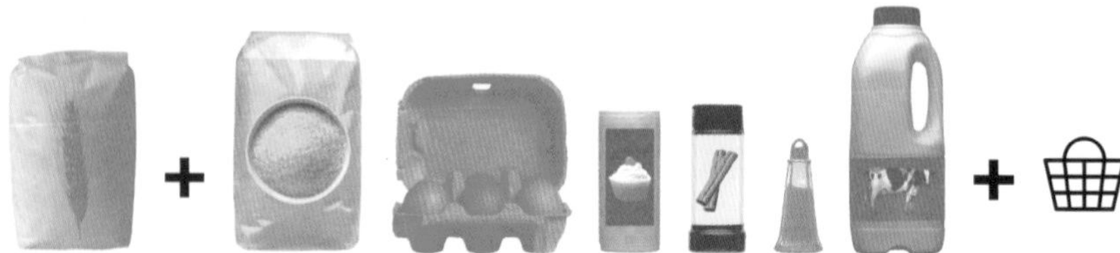

JAR OF PEANUT BUTTER

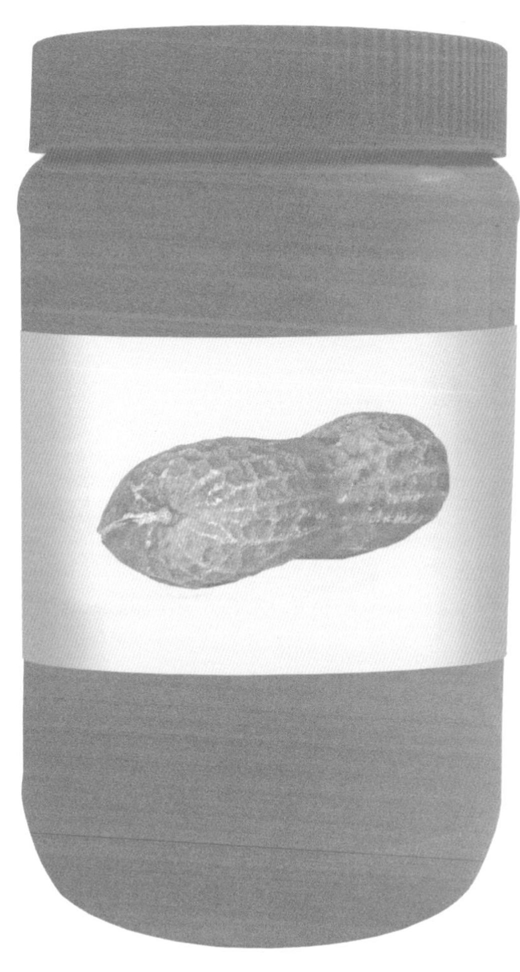

PEANUT BUTTER COOKIES (BASIC RECIPE)

MAKES ABOUT 25
PREPARATION TIME: 10 MINUTES
COOKING TIME: 10 MINUTES, PLUS COOLING

FROM THE STORE:
ROASTED SALTED PEANUTS

2 CUPS (9 OZ/250 G) ALL-PURPOSE (PLAIN) FLOUR
1 TEASPOON BAKING POWDER
¾ CUP (5 OZ/150 G) SUPERFINE (CASTER) SUGAR
½ CUP (2¾ OZ/75 G) ROASTED SALTED PEANUTS, COARSELY CHOPPED
SCANT ⅔ CUP (5 OZ/150 G) PEANUT BUTTER
2 EGGS, BEATEN
SCANT ½ CUP (3½ FL OZ/100 ML) MILK

Form this cookie dough into a sausage shape, wrap in plastic wrap (clingfilm), and chill until you want some cookies, or you can simply slice into disks and bake as many cookies as you need.

- To make the cookie dough, preheat the oven to 350°F/180°C/Gas mark 4 and line a baking sheet with parchment (baking) paper. Mix the flour, baking powder, and sugar together in large bowl, then add the peanuts, peanut butter, eggs, and milk and mix until smooth.
- Put about 25 heaping tablespoons of the mixture, ¾ inch/2 cm apart, onto the prepared sheet. Flatten slightly, then bake in the hot oven for about 10 minutes, or until golden brown. Cool on a wire rack.

 +   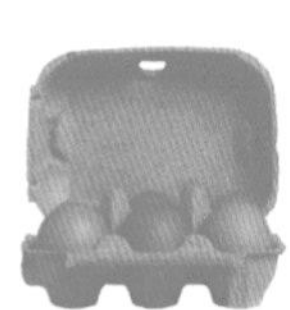  +

PEANUT BUTTER AND SESAME COOKIES

FROM THE STORE:
ROASTED SALTED PEANUTS
SESAME SEEDS

1 × PEANUT BUTTER COOKIES (BASIC RECIPE) INGREDIENTS
½ CUP (2¾ OZ/75 G) SESAME SEEDS

- Make the cookie dough as above, adding the sesame seeds to the dough mixture then bake and cool as in the basic recipe.

 +   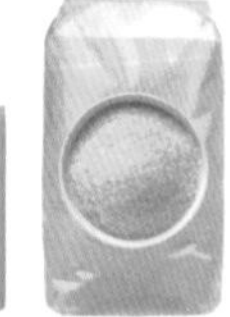 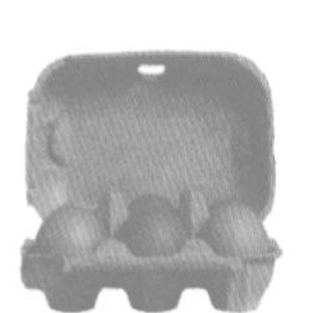  

PEANUT BUTTER AND CHOC CHIP COOKIES

FROM THE STORE:
ROASTED SALTED PEANUTS

1 × PEANUT BUTTER COOKIES (BASIC RECIPE) INGREDIENTS
3½ OZ/100 G BITTERSWEET (DARK) CHOCOLATE, CHOPPED

- Make the cookie dough as in the basic recipe opposite, stirring the chocolate into the dough mixture, then bake and cool as in the basic recipe.

 +    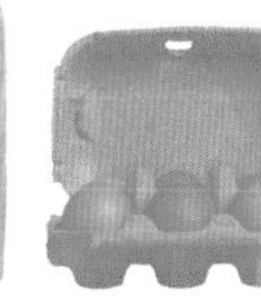   +

PEANUT BUTTER AND JELLY COOKIES

FROM THE STORE:
ROASTED SALTED PEANUTS
JELLY (JAM)

1 × PEANUT BUTTER COOKIES (BASIC RECIPE) INGREDIENTS
GENEROUS ⅓ CUP (4 OZ/120 G) JELLY (JAM)

- Make the dough as in the basic recipe opposite but instead of flattening the dough, press your thumb into the center of each cookie, then fill each with ½ teaspoon of your favorite jelly (jam) and bake and cool as in the basic recipe.

 +      +

BABY EGGPLANTS WITH SPICY PEANUT DRESSING

SERVES 2
PREPARATION TIME: 10 MINUTES
COOKING TIME: 5 MINUTES

FROM THE STORE:
BABY EGGPLANTS (AUBERGINES)
CILANTRO (CORIANDER)

8 BABY EGGPLANTS (AUBERGINES), HALVED LENGTHWISE
1 TABLESPOON OLIVE OIL, PLUS EXTRA TO DRIZZLE
HANDFUL CILANTRO (CORIANDER), LEAVES PICKED, TO SERVE
STEAMED WHITE BASMATI RICE, TO SERVE (OPTIONAL)

FOR THE DRESSING
2 TABLESPOONS PEANUT BUTTER
1 TABLESPOON SOY SAUCE
1 TABLESPOON WHITE WINE VINEGAR
1 CLOVE GARLIC, CRUSHED
½ TEASPOON SUPERFINE (CASTER) SUGAR
½ TEASPOON CHILI FLAKES
SALT AND FRESHLY GROUND BLACK PEPPER

TIP:
IF YOU CAN'T FIND BABY EGGPLANTS AT THE STORE, YOU CAN USE A LARGE EGGPLANT AND SIMPLY CUT IT INTO 2-INCH/5-CM LONG PIECES.

This is a great vegetarian barbecue dish; just grill the eggplants (aubergines) over coals. Any leftover dressing would be good with some grilled chicken, too.

- Mix all the dressing ingredients together in a small bowl with 2 tablespoons water and plenty of salt and pepper. Set aside.
- Heat the broiler (grill) to high. Put the eggplant (aubergine) halves onto a baking sheet and drizzle with the oil, turn to coat in the oil, then lay cut-side down on the sheet. Broil (grill) for 2–3 minutes until the skin is wrinkled and starting to char. Carefully flip the eggplant halves over and cook for another 2 minutes, or until the flesh is golden. Remove from the heat, season, and drizzle with a little extra oil.
- Transfer the eggplants to a serving plate, drizzle over the dressing, and let stand for 5 minutes before sprinkling with cilantro (coriander) and serving. These are perfect served with steamed rice.

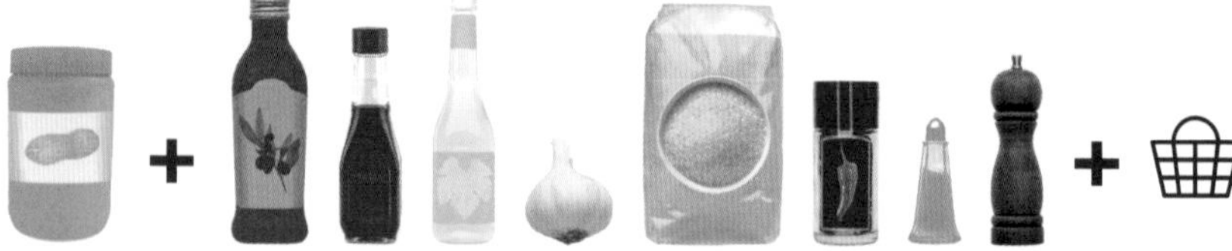

BANANA PANCAKES WITH PEANUT BUTTER AND BACON

SERVES 4
PREPARATION TIME: 10 MINUTES
COOKING TIME: 15–20 MINUTES

FROM THE STORE:
BANANAS
LEAN (STREAKY) BACON

SCANT 1¼ CUPS (5 OZ/140 G) ALL-PURPOSE (PLAIN) FLOUR
1 TEASPOON BAKING POWDER
PINCH OF SALT
½ TEASPOON GROUND CINNAMON
2 TABLESPOONS SUPERFINE (CASTER) SUGAR
3 BANANAS, 1 MASHED, 2 SLICED
2 TABLESPOONS PEANUT BUTTER, PLUS EXTRA TO SERVE
⅔ CUP (5 FL OZ/150 ML) MILK, PLUS A LITTLE EXTRA
2 EGGS, LIGHTLY BEATEN
1 TABLESPOON OLIVE OIL
8 SLICES (RASHERS) LEAN (STREAKY) BACON

There is no better brunch dish than this one. You can halve, double, or triple the quantity, depending on how many people you need to feed.

- Put the flour, baking powder, salt, cinnamon, and sugar into a bowl and whisk to combine. Make a little well in the center and set aside.
- In a separate bowl, mix the mashed banana, peanut butter, milk, and eggs until fully combined and smooth. Pour into the center of the flour well and mix, making sure there are no large lumps of banana in the batter.
- Heat the oil in a large skillet (frying pan) then preheat the oven to the lowest setting; you'll need to cook in batches, so the cooked pancakes can keep warm in the oven until ready to serve.
- Drop tablespoonfuls of the batter into the skillet, making pancakes about 3¼ inches/8 cm wide, and cook for 2–3 minutes until bubbles appear on the surface. Flip over and cook for another 1–2 minutes. Remove to a plate and keep warm in the oven. Repeat with the remaining mixture.
- Once the pancakes are cooked, quickly fry the bacon in the heated skillet until crisp.
- To serve, layer up the pancakes, starting with a pancake, then a little peanut butter, followed by some banana slices, then repeat the layers twice more. Add a dab more peanut butter loosened with a drop of milk if you like and top each stack with 2 slices of crispy bacon.

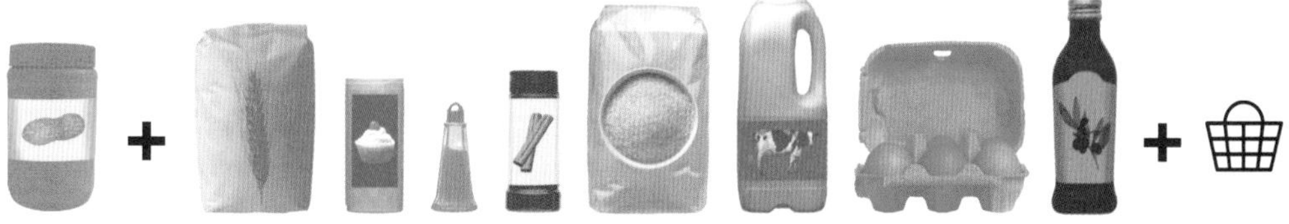

CHICKEN SATAY

SERVES 4
PREPARATION TIME: 10 MINUTES, PLUS 2 HOURS MARINATING
COOKING TIME: 20–25 MINUTES

FROM THE STORE:
LIMES
CHICKEN THIGHS

2 LIMES, 1 ZESTED AND JUICED AND 1 CUT INTO WEDGES, TO SERVE
2 CLOVES GARLIC, FINELY CHOPPED
1 TEASPOON SUPERFINE (CASTER) SUGAR
1 TABLESPOON SOY SAUCE
½ TEASPOON GROUND TURMERIC
1 TEASPOON CUMIN SEEDS, BASHED
½ TEASPOON CHILI FLAKES
4 TABLESPOONS PEANUT BUTTER
1 LB 2 OZ/500 G SKINLESS, BONELESS CHICKEN THIGHS, CUT INTO STRIPS
1 CUP (7 OZ/200 G) WHITE BASMATI RICE (OPTIONAL)
OLIVE OIL, FOR OILING
SCANT 1 CUP (7 FL OZ/200 ML) COCONUT MILK

You can serve the chicken and sauce by itself for an appetizer, or with the rice for a substantial main meal.

- In a bowl, mix the lime zest and juice with the garlic, sugar, soy sauce, turmeric, cumin, chili flakes, and peanut butter, then put half the sauce in a large bowl with the chicken strips. Cover with plastic wrap (clingfilm) and marinate in the refrigerator for 2 hours. Put the remaining sauce in a bowl and keep in the refrigerator until ready to use.
- At the same time, soak 12–15 bamboo skewers in cold water.
- Remove the chicken from the marinade, leaving on as much sauce as possible, then thread the chicken strips in an "S" shape onto the soaked skewers.
- Heat the broiler (grill) to medium-high, line a broiler (grill) tray with aluminum foil, and brush with a little oil. Put the skewers on the tray and broil (grill) them for 10–12 minutes until cooked through, turning halfway through.
- Cook the rice, if using, in a pan of boiling water for 8–10 minutes, or according to the package directions.
- Meanwhile, pour the remaining half of the sauce into a small pan with the coconut milk; if possible, try not to mix the cream at the top and milk at the bottom, and scoop the cream from the top into the pan, making the rest of the scant 1 cup (7 fl oz/200 ml) up with the coconut milk beneath. Gently heat through, then pour the sauce into dipping bowls and sprinkle with a few extra chili flakes.
- Serve the chicken skewers with the bowls of sauce on the side, spoonfuls of rice, if using, and lime wedges.

WEST AFRICAN PEANUT SOUP

SERVES 4
PREPARATION TIME: 10 MINUTES
COOKING TIME: 15 MINUTES

FROM THE STORE:
RED BELL PEPPER
BABY LEAF SPINACH

1 TABLESPOON OLIVE OIL
1 ONION, SLICED
1 RED BELL PEPPER, SEEDED AND SLICED
2 CLOVES GARLIC, CHOPPED
1 TEASPOON CHILI FLAKES
1 TEASPOON CUMIN SEEDS, BASHED
½ TEASPOON GROUND CINNAMON
1 × 14-OZ/400-G CAN CHOPPED TOMATOES
1 × 14-OZ/400-G CAN COCONUT MILK
1 BOUILLON (STOCK) CUBE
5 TABLESPOONS PEANUT BUTTER
1 × 3½-OZ/100-G BAG BABY LEAF SPINACH
SALT AND FRESHLY GROUND BLACK PEPPER

TIP:
STIR A 14-OZ/400-G CAN OF BLACK BEANS INTO THE SOUP INSTEAD OF THE SPINACH TO TURN IT INTO A WHOLESOME STEW.

This is the ultimate in quick and easy food. Tasty, warming, and satisfying, this soup can be on the table in less than 30 minutes.

- Heat the oil in a pan, add the onion and bell pepper, and cook over medium heat for 5 minutes, or until softened and starting to take on some color. Add the garlic, chili flakes, cumin, and cinnamon and cook for another 1 minute.
- Tip the tomatoes and coconut milk into the pan, crumble the bouillon (stock) cube into the empty tomato can, add scant ½ cup (3½ fl oz/100 ml) hot water, stir to dissolve, and then pour into the soup. Bring to a boil, then reduce the heat and simmer for 8 minutes. Stir in the peanut butter and the spinach and cook for a few minutes until the spinach has wilted. Add plenty of seasoning, ladle into bowls, and serve.

PEANUT BUTTER NOODLES WITH BROCCOLI

SERVES 2
PREPARATION TIME: 5 MINUTES
COOKING TIME: 5 MINUTES

FROM THE STORE:

DRIED EGG, UDON, OR WHOLE WHEAT NOODLES
PURPLE SPROUTING BROCCOLI OR ZUCCHINI (COURGETTE)

- 2 HEAPING TABLESPOONS PEANUT BUTTER
- 2 TABLESPOONS SOY SAUCE
- ½ TEASPOON CHILI FLAKES
- 1 TEASPOON WHITE WINE VINEGAR, PLUS EXTRA FOR THE ONION
- ½ TEASPOON SUPERFINE (CASTER) SUGAR, PLUS EXTRA FOR THE ONION
- 1 LARGE CLOVE GARLIC, FINELY CHOPPED
- ½ ONION, THINLY SLICED
- ½ TEASPOON SALT
- 2 NESTS DRIED EGG, UDON, OR WHOLE WHEAT NOODLES
- 7 OZ/200 G PURPLE SPROUTING BROCCOLI, SLICED IN HALF ON THE DIAGONAL, OR 1 LARGE ZUCCHINI (COURGETTE), CUT INTO RIBBONS

TIP:
THIS IS ALSO GREAT COLD IN LUNCHBOXES; ADD A DRIZZLE OF OIL TO LOOSEN IT UP IF IT HAS BEEN IN THE REFRIGERATOR.

This is an absolute staple in both the O'Sullivan and Reynolds households. You can replace the broccoli with some chopped cucumber, shredded carrot, or zucchini (courgette) ribbons, if you like.

- To make the sauce, mix the peanut butter with the soy sauce, chili flakes, vinegar, sugar, and garlic in a large bowl, then add about 3–4 tablespoons water, a little at a time, to loosen the sauce; it needs to be consistency of cream. Check the seasoning, adding more soy or sugar to adjust if necessary.
- Put the sliced onion into a separate bowl and pour over about 1 tablespoon vinegar and sprinkle over 1 teaspoon sugar and the salt to lightly pickle.
- Cook the noodles according to the package directions in a large pan of boiling water with the broccoli, drain, then add to the bowl with the sauce. (If using zucchini [courgette] serve it raw.)
- To serve, divide between 2 plates, then drain the pickled onions and sprinkle over the top.

CHOCOLATE AND PEANUT BUTTER FONDANTS

SERVES 4
PREPARATION TIME: 15 MINUTES
COOKING TIME: 10 MINUTES

FROM THE STORE:
VANILLA ICE CREAM
CARAMEL SAUCE

1 TABLESPOON OLIVE OIL, PLUS EXTRA FOR OILING
SCANT ½ CUP (3½ OZ/100 G) PEANUT BUTTER, AT ROOM TEMPERATURE
2¾ OZ/75 G BITTERSWEET (DARK) CHOCOLATE, COARSELY CHOPPED
2 EGGS
½ CUP (3½ OZ/100 G) SUPERFINE (CASTER) SUGAR
GENEROUS ⅓ CUP (2 OZ/50 G) ALL-PURPOSE (PLAIN) FLOUR

TO SERVE
VANILLA ICE CREAM
CARAMEL SAUCE

TIP:
IF YOU DON'T HAVE DARIOLE MOLDS OR RAMEKINS YOU COULD MAKE THE FONDANTS IN OVENPROOF TEA CUPS OR A MUFFIN PAN.

This is the dessert that will make you look like a much better cook than you may be. We whip these up on a regular basis, basking in the glory that their molten middles bring. Let's keep how easy these are between ourselves—we don't want anyone stealing our thunder.

- Preheat the oven to 400°F/200°C/Gas mark 6. Lightly oil 4 × 7-fl oz/200-ml dariole molds or ramekins and place on a baking sheet. If using ramekins, line the base of each ramekin with parchment (baking) paper.
- Put the oil, peanut butter, and chocolate into a small microwavable bowl and microwave in 20-second intervals, stirring after each one, until the mixture is smooth. Set aside. Alternatively, put the oil, chocolate, and peanut butter into a heatproof bowl set over a pan of gently simmering water, making sure the bottom of the bowl doesn't touch the water, and leave until the chocolate has melted. Remove from the heat and stir until smooth. Set aside.
- Whisk the eggs and sugar together in a bowl until pale and fluffy and almost doubled in volume. This will take about 5 minutes, so be patient. Stir a spoonful of this mixture into the melted chocolate and peanut butter to loosen, then carefully fold in the remaining beaten egg as efficiently as possible so as not to lose too much volume. Sift the flour over the mixture and carefully fold in. Spoon the mixture into the prepared molds.
- Bake in the hot oven for 8–10 minutes. The surface should be set but there will be a slight wobble if you poke the middle. Loosen the edges of each fondant with a knife, place a serving plate over the top of each one, flip the plate over, and carefully lift off the mold. Peel off the parchment paper, if using. Add a scoop of ice cream and a generous squeeze of caramel sauce, and serve immediately.

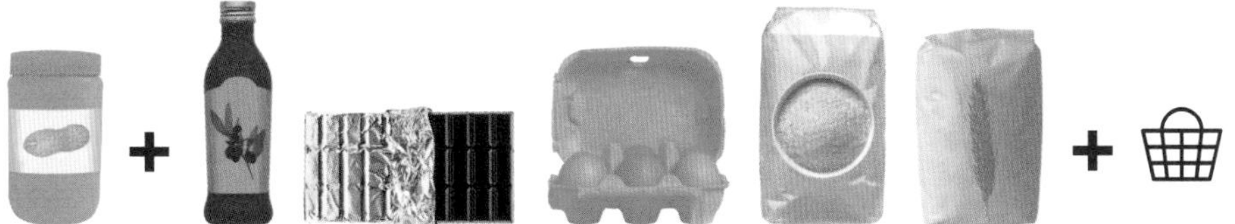

PEANUT BUTTER BLONDIES

MAKES 9
PREPARATION TIME: 10 MINUTES
COOKING TIME: 35 MINUTES, PLUS COOLING

FROM THE STORE:
WHITE CHOCOLATE
SALTED PEANUTS

OLIVE OIL, FOR OILING
GENEROUS ¾ CUP (7 OZ/200 G) PEANUT BUTTER
¾ CUP (5 OZ/150 G) SUPERFINE (CASTER) SUGAR
7 OZ/200 G WHITE CHOCOLATE, COARSELY CHOPPED
3 EGGS, LIGHTLY BEATEN
GENEROUS ¾ CUP (3½ OZ/100 G) ALL-PURPOSE (PLAIN) FLOUR
1 TEASPOON BAKING POWDER
⅓ CUP (2 OZ/50 G) SALTED PEANUTS, CHOPPED

This recipe will work just as well with milk or semisweet (plain) chocolate. The blondies can be stored in an airtight container for several days.

- Preheat the oven to 350°F/180°C/Gas mark 4 and oil and line an 8 × 8-inch/20 × 20-cm square baking pan with parchment (baking) paper.
- Put the peanut butter, sugar, and 5 oz/150 g of the chocolate into a large heatproof bowl. Set the bowl over a pan of gently simmering water, making sure the bottom of the bowl doesn't touch the water. Stir and heat until the chocolate has melted and the ingredients have combined, then remove from the heat. Allow to cool for a few minutes, then gradually add the eggs, beating after each addition, until fully combined.
- Sift the flour and baking powder together into a bowl, then fold into the wet ingredients. Scrape the blondie batter into the prepared pan, scatter over the remaining chocolate and the chopped peanuts. Bake in the hot oven for 25–30 minutes, or until just firm in the center with a harder crust around the edges. Allow to cool in the pan for a few minutes before transferring to a wire rack to cool to room temperature. Cut into squares and serve.

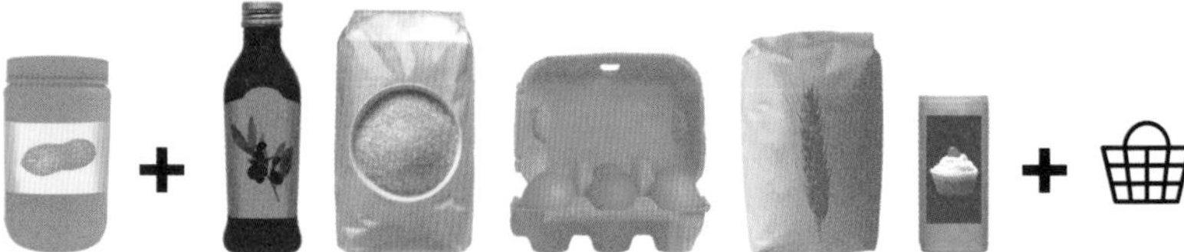

BOX OF EGGS

FRITTATA (BASIC RECIPE)

SERVES 2
PREPARATION TIME: 10 MINUTES
COOKING TIME: 10 MINUTES

1 TABLESPOON OLIVE OIL
1 ONION, THINLY SLICED
4 EGGS, BEATEN
SPLASH OF MILK
SALT AND GROUND BLACK PEPPER

Everyone loves a frittata, right? Especially with the following ideas for simple fillings.

- To make the frittata base, preheat the broiler (grill) to high. Heat the oil in small skillet (frying pan), then add the onion and cook over medium heat for 5–10 minutes until softened.
- Whisk the eggs with a splash of milk in a medium bowl. Add the filling of your choice to the skillet, followed by the eggs. Season with salt and pepper. Swirl the skillet to make sure the egg mixture is well distributed, cook for 5 minutes, to set the bottom, then cook under a hot broiler for 2–3 minutes to set the top.

POTATO AND WATERCRESS FRITTATA

FROM THE STORE:
NEW POTATOES
WATERCRESS

1 × FRITTATA (BASIC RECIPE) INGREDIENTS
14 OZ/400 G COOKED NEW POTATOES, SLICED
1 × 3-OZ/80-G BAG WATERCRESS, COARSELY CHOPPED

- Make the frittata base as above, adding the potatoes and watercress to the skillet once the onion has softened. Fry for about 2 minutes to brown the potatoes and wilt the watercress. Reduce the heat a little and add the egg mixture. Cook as above.

BACON AND GRUYÈRE FRITTATA

FROM THE STORE:
SMOKED BACON PIECES (LARDONS) OR PANCETTA
GRUYÈRE CHEESE

1 × FRITTATA (BASIC RECIPE) INGREDIENTS
3½ OZ/100 G SMOKED BACON PIECES (LARDONS) OR PANCETTA
3½ OZ/100 G GRUYÈRE CHEESE, GRATED

- Make the frittata base as opposite, frying the smoked bacon pieces (lardons) or pancetta with the onion for 5 minutes until golden. Mix half of the Gruyère with the eggs and milk, reduce the heat and pour the mixture over the bacon and onions, then sprinkle over the remaining cheese. Cook as opposite until the cheese is bubbling and golden.

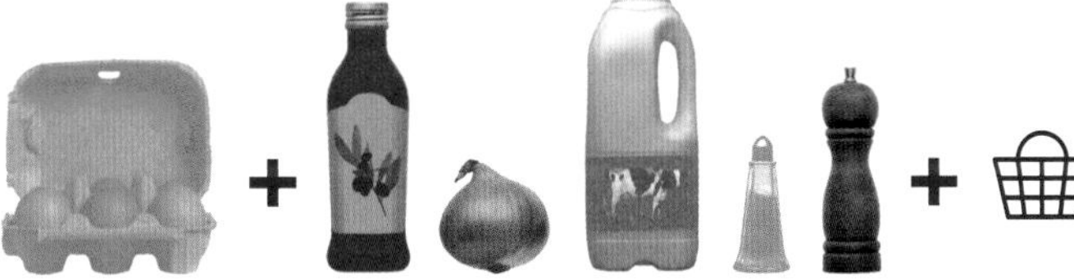

SMOKED SALMON AND SOFT CHEESE FRITTATA

FROM THE STORE:
SMOKED SALMON
GARLIC AND HERB SOFT CHEESE

1 × FRITTATA (BASIC RECIPE) INGREDIENTS
3½ OZ/100 G SMOKED SALMON, TORN INTO PIECES
5 OZ/150 G GARLIC AND HERB SOFT CHEESE
1 TABLESPOON MILK

- Make the frittata base as opposite, mixing three-quarters of the smoked salmon into the egg mixture, reduce the heat a little and then add to the skillet. In a bowl, mix the soft cheese and milk together to loosen the cheese, then swirl into the eggs and salmon. Top with the remaining smoked salmon and cook as opposite.

CARAMELIZED ONION AND GOAT CHEESE TART

SERVES 4–6
PREPARATION TIME: 10 MINUTES
COOKING TIME: 30 MINUTES, PLUS COOLING

FROM THE STORE:
READY-ROLLED PUFF PASTRY
SOFT GOAT CHEESE

1 × 11¼-OZ/320-G PACKAGE READY-ROLLED PUFF PASTRY
2 TABLESPOONS OLIVE OIL
2 ONIONS, THINLY SLICED
2 CLOVES GARLIC, CHOPPED
1 TABLESPOON SUPERFINE (CASTER) SUGAR
1 TABLESPOON WHITE WINE VINEGAR
11 OZ/300 G RINDLESS GOAT CHEESE, CRUMBLED
3 EGGS, LIGHTLY BEATEN
SALT AND FRESHLY GROUND BLACK PEPPER

If you have people coming around, this makes either a casual but smart veggie main, or a suitably fancy appetizer or canapé, cut into squares.

- Preheat the oven to 400°F/200°C/Gas mark 6.
- Unroll the pastry and lay on a baking sheet. Use a sharp knife to make a ¾-inch/2-cm border around the edge of the pastry—be careful not to cut all the way through the pastry. Prick inside of the border with the knife and bake in the hot oven for 15 minutes, or until golden and risen.
- Meanwhile, heat the oil in a large nonstick skillet (frying pan) over medium heat, add the onions and fry for about 8 minutes, or until softened and turning golden. Add the garlic, sugar, and vinegar with plenty of seasoning and cook for 2 minutes, or until the onions are deep golden in color and sticky. Remove from the heat.
- Remove the pastry from the oven and use the back of a spoon to flatten the center, then spread the onion mixture loosely over the pastry. Beat three-quarters of the goat cheese with the eggs, then pour over the onions. Dot with the remaining goat cheese, then return to the oven for 15 minutes, or until the egg is set and the pastry golden and well risen.
- Remove from the oven and cool for 10 minutes before slicing and serving.

EGG AND ANCHOVY SALAD

SERVES 2
PREPARATION TIME: 10 MINUTES
COOKING TIME: 15 MINUTES

FROM THE STORE:
CRUSTY LOAF OF BREAD
BABY BOSTON (BABY GEM) LETTUCE

4 EGGS
2 TABLESPOONS OLIVE OIL
1 CLOVE GARLIC, BASHED WITH THE FLAT OF A KNIFE
3 SLICES BREAD FROM A CRUSTY LOAF, CUBED
1 BABY BOSTON (BABY GEM) LETTUCE, BROKEN INTO LEAVES
8 ANCHOVY FILLETS, HALVED LENGTHWISE

FOR THE DRESSING
2 TABLESPOONS OLIVE OIL
2 TABLESPOONS WHITE WINE VINEGAR
1 TEASPOON WHOLE GRAIN MUSTARD
½ CLOVE GARLIC, CRUSHED

TIP:
FOR SOME EXTRA PROTEIN, REPLACE THE CROUTONS WITH BROILED (GRILLED) CHICKEN SLICES IF YOU LIKE.

This salad is the perfect lunch or light midweek meal.

- Cook the eggs in a pan of boiling water for 6 minutes, drain, and run under cold water to stop them from cooking further. Shell and set aside.
- Heat the oil in a large nonstick skillet (frying pan), add the garlic, and sizzle over medium heat for a few seconds. Tip in the bread cubes and fry for 8 minutes, stirring frequently until the cubes are golden and crisp. Drain on paper towels and discard the garlic.
- Mix all the dressing ingredients together in a small bowl. Add the lettuce leaves and toss to coat in the dressing.
- To assemble the salad, pile the leaves onto 2 plates, lay the anchovy fillets over the top, give each person a couple of eggs cut in half, and plenty of crunchy croutons. Serve immediately.

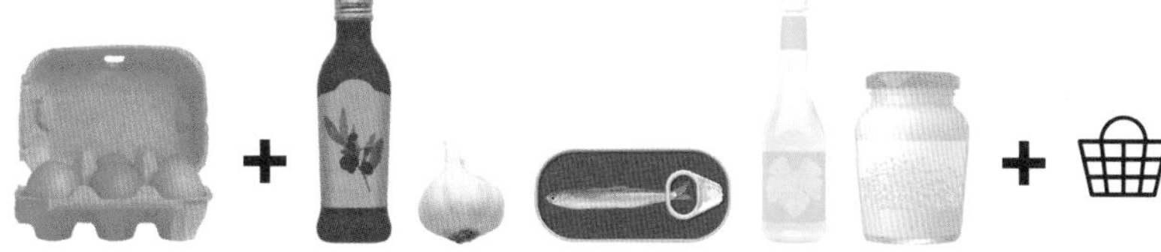

HAM AND EGGS WITH SCALLION DRESSING

SERVES 2
PREPARATION TIME: 5 MINUTES
COOKING TIME: 10 MINUTES

FROM THE STORE:
HAND-CARVED HAM
SCALLIONS (SPRING ONIONS)

7 OZ/200 G HAND-CARVED HAM OR 4 THICK SLICES
2 TABLESPOONS OLIVE OIL
2 EGGS

FOR THE DRESSING
2 TABLESPOONS OLIVE OIL
1 BUNCH SCALLIONS (SPRING ONIONS), COARSELY CHOPPED
2 TABLESPOONS WHITE WINE VINEGAR
2 TEASPOONS WHOLE GRAIN MUSTARD
SALT AND FRESHLY GROUND BLACK PEPPER

This is a quick and easy take on eggs Benedict without the fuss of hollandaise sauce. It's perfect for breakfast or a light lunch. Use the best ham you can afford, as the results will be even more satisfying.

- To make the dressing, heat 1 tablespoon of the oil in a large nonstick skillet (frying pan), add the scallions (spring onions) and cook over high heat for 1 minute, then tip them out into a small bowl and add the remaining oil and the vinegar and mustard. Season and stir to combine. Set aside.
- Divide the ham between 2 plates and leave until it is at room temperature. Put the skillet back over the heat, add 1 tablespoon of the oil, then crack 2 eggs into the hot oil and fry until the edges are crisp and the yolks are cooked to your liking.
- Transfer the eggs to the plates with the ham and serve with the scallion dressing spooned over the top.

ZUCCHINI AND BASIL MUFFINS

MAKES 12
PREPARATION TIME: 10 MINUTES
COOKING TIME: 20–25 MINUTES,
PLUS COOLING

FROM THE STORE:
ZUCCHINI (COURGETTES)
BASIL

2 TEASPOONS BAKING POWDER
1¾ CUPS (8 OZ/225 G) ALL-PURPOSE (PLAIN) FLOUR
½ TEASPOON CHILI FLAKES
½ TEASPOON SALT
1 LARGE OR 2 SMALL ZUCCHINI (COURGETTES), GRATED
3–4 TABLESPOONS SHREDDED BASIL LEAVES
¾ CUP (6 FL OZ/175 ML) MILK
1 EGG, BEATEN
SCANT ¼ CUP (1¾ FL OZ/50 ML) OLIVE OIL
GROUND BLACK PEPPER

TIP:
IF YOU'VE STORED THE MUFFINS IN A PLASTIC CONTAINER FOR A FEW DAYS, CUT THEM IN HALF LENGTHWISE, TOAST OR BROIL (GRILL), AND SERVE WARM.

These savory muffins are perfect for lunch boxes, as well as being brilliant when served with soup, such as Cream of Tomato Soup on page 75.

- Preheat the oven to 400°F/200°C/Gas mark 6. Line a 12-section muffin pan with paper liners (cases).
- Sift together the baking powder and flour into a large bowl, add the chili flakes and salt and season generously with pepper. Add the zucchini (courgette) and basil and stir to combine.
- In another bowl, mix the milk, egg, and oil together. Pour into the dry mixture, working quickly so as to only just combine the ingredients. Drop spoonfuls of the batter into the muffin liners, filling to two-thirds full, then cook in the hot oven for 20–25 minutes, or until risen and golden. Cool on a wire rack.

FRENCH TOAST WITH ROASTED BLACK PEPPER STRAWBERRIES

SERVES 2
PREPARATION TIME: 10 MINUTES
COOKING TIME: 10 MINUTES

FROM THE STORE:
THICK-SLICED BREAD
STRAWBERRIES

FOR THE STRAWBERRIES
1¾ CUPS (9 OZ/250 G) STRAWBERRIES, HULLED AND HALVED
2 TEASPOONS SUPERFINE (CASTER) SUGAR
FRESHLY GROUND BLACK PEPPER

FOR THE FRENCH TOAST
2 EGGS
1 TABLESPOON MILK
2 TEASPOONS SUPERFINE (CASTER) SUGAR
TINY PINCH OF SALT
2 SLICES GOOD-QUALITY, THICK-SLICED BREAD
1 TABLESPOON OLIVE OIL

TIP:
IF PEACHES ARE IN SEASON, TRY USING 2 SLICED PEACHES WITH BLACK PEPPER INSTEAD OF STRAWBERRIES.

This is a summer weekend classic for us with good reason; the black pepper on the strawberries adds a little heat and contrast to the intensely sweet fruit and rich toast.

- Preheat the oven to 400°F/200°C/Gas mark 6 and line a baking sheet with parchment (baking) paper.
- Mix the strawberries and sugar together in a large bowl and leave to macerate for 5 minutes, then spread out over the prepared baking sheet. Grind over a decent amount of black pepper, then roast in the hot oven for 10 minutes, or until the strawberries are softened and sticky.
- Meanwhile, make the French toast. Whisk the eggs, milk, sugar, and salt together in large shallow bowl, then dip the slices of bread into the mixture, making sure each side is well coated.
- Put the oil in a large skillet (frying pan) over medium heat, take the bread out of the egg mixture and fry until golden, about 2 minutes on each side. Serve with the strawberries.

YEAR-ROUND SUMMER BERRY PAVLOVA

SERVES 6
PREPARATION TIME: 15 MINUTES
COOKING TIME: 1 HOUR, PLUS COOLING

FROM THE STORE:
HEAVY (DOUBLE) CREAM
FROZEN SUMMER BERRIES

3 EGG WHITES
¾ CUP (5 OZ/150 G) SUPERFINE (CASTER) SUGAR

FOR THE FILLING
SCANT 2 CUPS (15 FL OZ/450 ML) HEAVY (DOUBLE) CREAM
11 OZ/300 G FROZEN SUMMER BERRIES, DEFROSTED
4 TABLESPOONS SUPERFINE (CASTER) SUGAR

TIP:
UNFILLED MERINGUE WILL KEEP IN AN AIRTIGHT CONTAINER FOR A WEEK, SO YOU CAN MAKE IT IN ADVANCE.

Frozen berries are very useful—throw them into a smoothie, blend them with yogurt into a cheat's ice cream, or layer under a crumble topping. They are cheaper than buying fresh berries and available all year round. Pavlova is so easy to make, the main appeal is that you can top it with any fruit you have in your fruit bowl. If you can't find heavy (double) cream you can always substitute it for thick Greek yogurt.

- Preheat the oven to 325°F/160°C/Gas mark 3. Line a baking sheet with parchment (baking) paper and draw a circle on the paper, about 8 inches/20 cm in diameter—a plate will help—then flip the paper over so it's pen/pencil side down. Set aside.
- Put the egg whites into a large clean bowl and whisk to stiff, shiny peaks—making sure they don't go grainy. Gradually add the sugar, a tablespoon at a time, beating after each addition to dissolve the sugar. Continue to whisk until the whites are super shiny and stiff. Use a large metal spoon to dollop the whites onto the parchment paper, filling the inside of the circle with meringue. Smooth the meringue with the back of the spoon and form a slight border around the edge with the tip of the spoon.
- Reduce the oven temperature to 275°F/140°C/Gas mark 1 and cook the meringue for 1 hour, or until puffed and lightly golden in color. Switch the oven off and let the meringue cool completely in the oven.
- Whip the cream to soft peaks in a bowl and set aside.
- Put the berries in a strainer (sieve) set over a bowl. Mix the sugar into the collected juice and set aside.
- Put the meringue onto a serving plate, dollop over the cream, then top with the berries. Spoon the sweetened juices over the top and serve immediately.

APPLE CAKE WITH VANILLA ICE CREAM

SERVES 6
PREPARATION TIME: 15 MINUTES
COOKING TIME: 50–60 MINUTES, PLUS COOLING

FROM THE STORE:

APPLES
VANILLA ICE CREAM

SCANT ½ CUP (3½ FL OZ/100 ML) OLIVE OIL, PLUS EXTRA FOR OILING
2 EGGS, LIGHTLY BEATEN
SCANT 1 CUP (6 OZ/175 G) SUPERFINE (CASTER) SUGAR, PLUS EXTRA FOR SPRINKLING
3 SMALL APPLES, 1 GRATED, 2 CORED AND THINLY SLICED
1⅔ CUPS (7 OZ/200 G) ALL-PURPOSE (PLAIN) FLOUR
2 TEASPOONS BAKING POWDER
1 TEASPOON GROUND CINNAMON
PINCH OF SALT
VANILLA ICE CREAM, TO SERVE

TIP:
SWAP THE APPLE FOR PEAR AND THE CINNAMON FOR WARMING GINGER. IT WILL PRODUCE A CAKE THAT IS PERFECT SERVED WITH CUSTARD RATHER THAN ICE CREAM.

This is a super-simple bake; the apples can be substituted for pears or even carrots, and you can add different spices depending on your mood and the seasons.

- Preheat the oven to 350°F/180°C/Gas mark 4 and oil and line the bottom of an 8-inch/20-cm round springform cake pan with parchment (baking) paper.
- Mix the oil, eggs, sugar, and grated apple together in a large bowl. Add the flour, baking powder, cinnamon, and salt and stir everything together until well combined. Scrape the cake batter into the prepared pan and smooth the surface with the back of a spoon. Lay the apple slices in circles around the top of the cake and sprinkle with more sugar. Bake in the hot oven for 50–60 minutes, or until well risen, golden, and a skewer inserted into the center of the cake comes out clean.
- Check the cake after 30 minutes, if it looks like it is taking on too much color, cover loosely with aluminum foil and continue cooking. Once cooked, remove from the oven and allow to cool for 10 minutes in the pan before transferring to a wire rack. Serve slightly warm with vanilla ice cream.

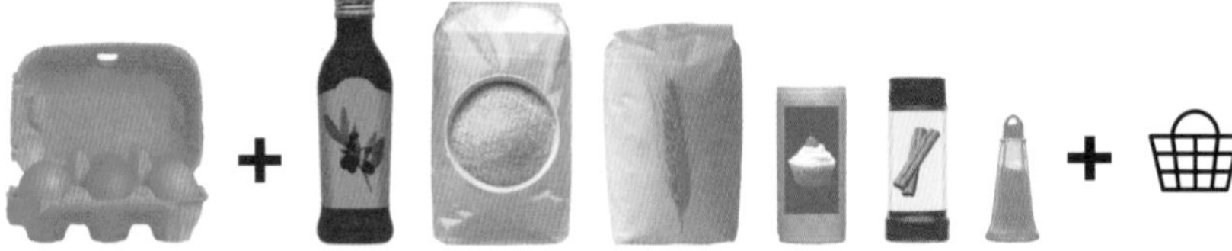

BAG OF PASTA

MAC AND CHEESE (BASIC RECIPE)

SERVES 4
PREPARATION TIME: 15 MINUTES
COOKING TIME: 35–40 MINUTES

2½ CUPS (20 FL OZ/600 ML) MILK
2 TABLESPOONS ALL-PURPOSE (PLAIN) FLOUR
3 TABLESPOONS OLIVE OIL
1 TEASPOON WHOLE GRAIN MUSTARD
14 OZ/400 G SHORT PASTA, SUCH AS MACARONI OR PENNE
SALT AND FRESHLY GROUND BLACK PEPPER

The ideal pasta for mac and cheese is of course macaroni, but it will taste just as good with any short pasta, like penne or fusilli.

- Preheat the oven to 350°F/180°C/Gas mark 4.
- To make the sauce, pour the milk into a pan and add the flour, oil, mustard, and salt and pepper. Whisk constantly over medium heat for 8–10 minutes until thick and smooth.
- Meanwhile, cook the pasta in a pan of boiling salted water for about 8 minutes, or according to the package directions, until almost done, then drain.
- Add your chosen cheeses and toppings to the sauce, add the pasta and mix well. Tip into an ovenproof baking dish and bake in the hot oven for 25–30 minutes until golden and bubbling.

 + 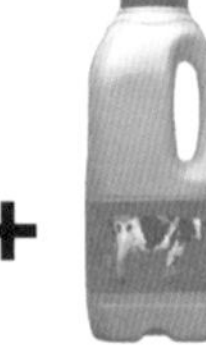     +

HERBY BREAD CRUMB AND PARMESAN MAC AND CHEESE

FROM THE STORE:
ITALIANPARMESAN CHEESE
ITALIAN HERB BREAD CRUMBS

1 × MAC AND CHEESE (BASIC RECIPE) INGREDIENTS
1¼ CUPS (3½ OZ/100 G) GRATED ITALIAN PARMESAN CHEESE
2¾ OZ/75 G ITALIAN HERB BREAD CRUMBS

- Follow the basic recipe for mac and cheese (above), adding half of the Parmesan to the sauce, then mix with the pasta. Mix the remaining Parmesan with the bread crumbs. Tip the pasta into an ovenproof dish, top with the bread crumb mixture, and bake as above.

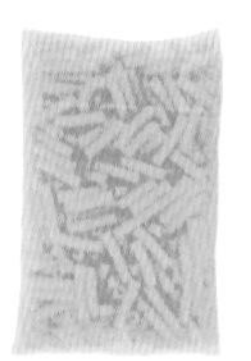 +  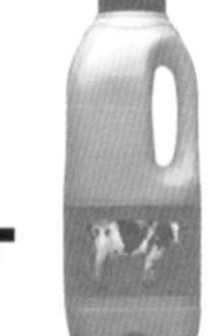      + 

CHEDDAR AND JALAPEÑO MAC AND CHEESE

FROM THE STORE:
CHEDDAR CHEESE
SLICED JALAPEÑOS

1 × MAC AND CHEESE (BASIC RECIPE) INGREDIENTS
1⅔ CUPS (7 OZ/200 G) GRATED CHEDDAR CHEESE
3 TABLESPOONS SLICED JALAPEÑOS

- Follow the basic recipe for mac and cheese (opposite), mixing three-quarters of the cheese with the sauce, then mix with the pasta and jalapeños. Tip the pasta into an ovenproof dish, sprinkle with the remaining cheese, and bake as opposite.

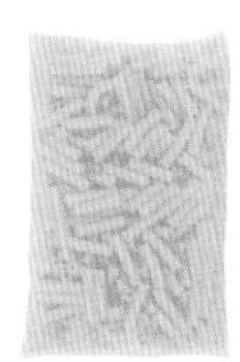 + 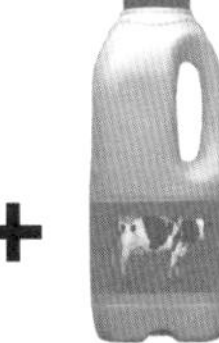 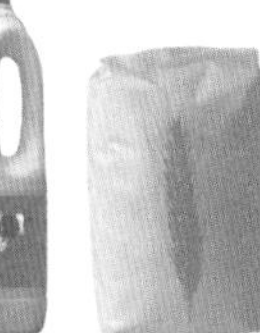    + 

BLUE CHEESE, ONION, AND THYME MAC AND CHEESE

FROM THE STORE:
THYME LEAVES
BLUE CHEESE

1 × MAC AND CHEESE (BASIC RECIPE) INGREDIENTS
OLIVE OIL, FOR FRYING
1 ONION, SLICED
2 TABLESPOONS THYME LEAVES, PLUS EXTRA TO SPRINKLE
5 OZ/150 G BLUE CHEESE, CRUMBLED

- Heat the oil in a pan, add the onion and thyme leaves, and fry over medium heat for 10 minutes, or until soft.
- Follow the basic recipe for mac and cheese (opposite), adding the onion and thyme mixture and half the blue cheese to the sauce. Mix with the pasta, then tip into an ovenproof dish, sprinkle with the remaining cheese, and bake as opposite.
- Serve sprinkled with a few extra thyme leaves.

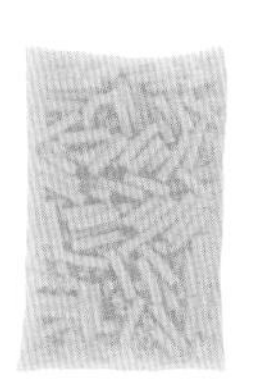 +          + 

PASTA WITH MUSSELS, GARLIC, AND PARSLEY

SERVES 2
PREPARATION TIME: 15 MINUTES
COOKING TIME: 15 MINUTES

FROM THE STORE:
MUSSELS
FLAT-LEAF PARSLEY

1 LB 2 OZ/500 G MUSSELS, CLEANED
5 OZ/150 G LONG PASTA, SUCH AS SPAGHETTI OR LINGUINE
1 TABLESPOON OLIVE OIL
1 ONION, FINELY CHOPPED
2 CLOVES GARLIC, FINELY CHOPPED
¼ BOUILLON (STOCK) CUBE MADE UP TO SCANT ½ CUP (3½ FL OZ/100 ML) BROTH (STOCK) WITH BOILING WATER
LARGE HANDFUL FLAT-LEAF PARSLEY, FINELY CHOPPED

TIP:
ADD A 14-OZ/400-G CAN CHOPPED TOMATOES TO THE SAUCE TO BULK IT OUT AND MAKE IT GO FURTHER. IF YOU ARE THINKING OF ENJOYING A GLASS OF WINE WITH THIS DISH, ADD A SPLASH TO THE PAN WITH THE BROTH (STOCK), IT WON'T BE WASTED.

If you can't find fresh mussels you can cheat and use a vacuum pack of mussels in garlic butter sauce. Simply cook the mussels according to the package directions and then toss through the cooked pasta. Don't tell anyone we told you that though!

- First, clean the mussels by scrubbing any dirt and barnacles from the shells, removing the strands of seaweed, and throwing away any with broken shells.
- Cook the pasta in a large pan of boiling salted water for 10 minutes, or according to the package directions, until al dente. Drain well.
- Meanwhile, heat the oil in a large pan with a tight-fitting lid, add the onion, and cook over medium heat for 5 minutes, or until the onion is soft but not colored. Add the garlic and cook for another 1 minute. Increase the heat, tip in the mussels, and stir to coat in the onion and garlic. Pour in the broth (stock), cover with the lid, and cook for 5 minutes, shaking the pan from time to time until all the mussels are opened. Discard any mussels that remain closed.
- Add the pasta and parsley to the pan and toss through the mussels. Ladle the pasta and any juices into bowls and serve immediately.

BASIL AND AVOCADO PASTA

SERVES 2
PREPARATION TIME: 5 MINUTES
COOKING TIME: 10 MINUTES

FROM THE STORE:
AVOCADO
BASIL

1 LARGE AVOCADO, PITTED AND PEELED
½ BUNCH BASIL, SHREDDED, PLUS A FEW LEAVES TO GARNISH
3 TABLESPOONS OLIVE OIL
1 CLOVE GARLIC, CHOPPED
11 OZ/300 G LONG PASTA, SUCH AS SPAGHETTI OR LINGUINE
SALT AND FRESHLY GROUND BLACK PEPPER

This sauce sounds unusual, but the creamy avocado and fragrant basil make for an indulgent pasta dish without adding meat or dairy. This works best with spaghetti, but is great with short pasta, too.

- Put the avocado, basil, oil, garlic, and a generous amount of salt and pepper into a food processor and blend until smooth.
- Cook the pasta in a pan of boiling salted water for a minute less than the package directions, drain then return to the pan with the sauce and gently heat through over low heat for 1 minute. Divide between 2 bowls and serve topped with the basil leaves and a little more black pepper, if you like.

ITALIAN SAUSAGE RAGU

SERVES 4
PREPARATION TIME: 10 MINUTES
COOKING TIME: 40 MINUTES

FROM THE STORE:
LUGANIGA ITALIAN SAUSAGE OR CHIPOLATAS
ITALIAN PARMESAN CHEESE

1 TABLESPOON OLIVE OIL
1 LUGANIGA ITALIAN SAUSAGE, IF YOU CAN FIND IT, CUT INTO 1 INCH/2.5 CM LENGTHS OR 8 CHIPOLATAS, CUT INTO 1 INCH/2.5 CM LENGTHS
2 ONIONS, THINLY SLICED
2 CLOVES GARLIC, CHOPPED
1 TEASPOON DRIED OREGANO
½ TEASPOON CHILI FLAKES
2 × 14-OZ/400-G CANS CHOPPED TOMATOES
14 OZ/400 G PASTA, WE USED PAPARDELLE BUT USE WHATEVER YOU HAVE
GRATED ITALIAN PARMESAN CHEESE, TO SERVE, (OPTIONAL)

TIP:
THIS IS A PERFECT FREEZER-FRIENDLY DISH. MAKE A DOUBLE QUANTITY AND FREEZE HALF FOR ANOTHER DAY. IT CAN BE FROZEN FOR UP TO 3–4 MONTHS.

Use good-quality sausages from a butcher if you can find them and if they are within your budget. A good sausage will be packed full of spices and great flavor, which means you don't have to add too much to the mix to achieve a great taste.

- Heat the oil in a large high-sided skillet (frying pan). Add the sausages and cook over medium heat for about 10 minutes until they are browned all over. Throw in the onions and garlic and cook in the sausage juices for about 8 minutes, or until soft. Add the oregano, chili flakes, and tomatoes, bring to a boil, reduce the heat, and simmer for 20 minutes, or until the sauce is thick and reduced.
- Meanwhile, cook the pasta in a large pan of boiling salted water for 10 minutes, or according to the package directions, until al dente. Drain well. Toss the pasta through the sauce and serve with grated Parmesan, if you like.

CLASSIC CARBONARA

SERVES 2
PREPARATION TIME: 5 MINUTES
COOKING TIME: 15 MINUTES

FROM THE STORE:
ITALIAN PARMESAN CHEESE
DRY-CURED SMOKED LEAN (STREAKY) BACON

11 OZ/300 G LONG PASTA, SUCH AS SPAGHETTI OR LINGUINE
3 EGGS
SCANT ⅔ CUP (2 OZ/50 G) FINELY GRATED ITALIAN PARMESAN CHEESE, PLUS EXTRA FOR SERVING (OPTIONAL)
1 TABLESPOON OLIVE OIL
8 SLICES (RASHERS) DRY-CURED SMOKED LEAN (STREAKY) BACON, FINELY CHOPPED
1 CLOVE GARLIC, CHOPPED
SALT AND FRESHLY GROUND BLACK PEPPER

TIP:
BUY THE BEST BACON YOU CAN AFFORD BECAUSE IT WILL IMPROVE THE FLAVOR OF THE DISH. THIS IS ALSO GREAT SERVED WITH SOME ANCHOVY CRUMBS (SEE PAGE 149) IF YOU HAVE SOME LEFTOVER.

Simple, classic, and oh so comforting, once you have mastered this dish you will turn to it over and over again for a speedy supper option.

- Cook the pasta in a large pan of boiling salted water for 10 minutes, or according to the package directions, until al dente. Drain, reserving ½ cup (4 fl oz/120 ml) of the pasta cooking water. Set aside.
- Lightly beat the eggs in a bowl with a fork, then add the Parmesan, and mix to combine. Add plenty of black pepper and a little salt—remember the bacon and Parmesan are salty. Set aside.
- Meanwhile, heat the oil in a large nonstick skillet (frying pan), add the bacon, and cook over medium heat for 5–8 minutes until golden and starting to crisp. Add the garlic and fry for 1 minute in the bacon fat, making sure it doesn't burn.
- Add the cooked pasta to the skillet, toss in the bacon and garlic oil to coat, and heat through. Remove the pan from the heat. Pour in the egg and cheese mixture and toss to coat—tongs are really useful for this. The heat of the pasta will cook and thicken the egg mixture. Add a splash of the reserved pasta cooking water and continue to toss the pasta until the sauce just clings to the outside of the strands—it should look like light (single) cream.
- Serve immediately with extra grated Parmesan, if you like.

BROCCOLI PASTA WITH SPICY ANCHOVY CRUMBS

SERVES 4
PREPARATION TIME: 5 MINUTES
COOKING TIME: 15 MINUTES

FROM THE STORE:
BROCCOLI
CRUSTY BREAD ROLL

- 12 OZ/350 G SHORT PASTA, SUCH AS ORECCHIETTE
- 1 HEAD BROCCOLI, CUT INTO BITE-SIZE FLORETS
- 3 TABLESPOONS OLIVE OIL, PLUS A GLUG
- 8 ANCHOVY FILLETS, COARSELY CHOPPED
- 2 CLOVES GARLIC, CHOPPED
- 1 TEASPOON CHILI FLAKES
- 1 CRUSTY BREAD ROLL, PROCESSED INTO CRUMBS
- SALT AND FRESHLY GROUND BLACK PEPPER

TIP:
USE GRATED ZUCCHINI (COURGETTE) IF YOU DON'T HAVE ANY BROCCOLI. SIMPLY COOK THE PASTA ACCORDING TO THE PACKAGE DIRECTIONS AND FRY THE GRATED ZUCCHINI WITH THE SECOND CLOVE OF GARLIC BEFORE TOSSING THROUGH THE COOKED PASTA.

This dish is traditionally made with turnip greens, which are coarsely chopped and cooked with the pasta; you could use the leafy tops of any vegetables such as beets (beetroots) or carrots. We have used broccoli as an alternative; the trick is to cook the broccoli until it is so soft that it breaks down and almost melts into the pasta.

- Cook the pasta and broccoli in a large pan of boiling salted water for about 10 minutes, or until the pasta is al dente and the broccoli is really soft. Drain, reserving ½ cup (4 fl oz/120 ml) of the cooking water.
- Meanwhile, heat 1½ tablespoons of the oil in a large nonstick skillet (frying pan) over medium heat. Add the anchovies and use a wooden spoon to break up the fillets, then stir in half the garlic, the chili flakes, and bread crumbs, and fry, stirring frequently, for 5 minutes until the crumbs are golden and crisp. Tip out onto a plate and put the skillet back on the heat.
- Heat the remaining oil in the skillet, add the remaining garlic, and sizzle for a few seconds over medium heat, then tip in the pasta and broccoli, add a splash of the reserved cooking water and an extra glug of oil, and shake the pan to coat the pasta in the garlicky sauce. Season, then divide among plates and sprinkle over the crisp anchovy crumbs.

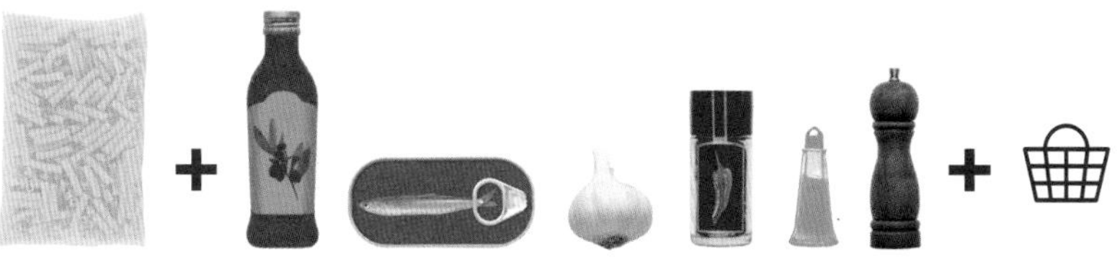

EGGPLANT PASTA PIE

SERVES 6
PREPARATION TIME: 30 MINUTES
COOKING TIME: 1 HOUR

FROM THE STORE:
EGGPLANTS (AUBERGINES)
MOZZARELLA CHEESE

1 TABLESPOON OLIVE OIL, PLUS EXTRA FOR BRUSHING
1 LARGE ONION, FINELY CHOPPED
3 CLOVES GARLIC, FINELY CHOPPED
6–8 ANCHOVY FILLETS, WITH THEIR OIL
2 × 14-OZ/400-G CANS CHOPPED TOMATOES
½ TEASPOON CHILI FLAKES
1 TEASPOON DRIED OREGANO
1 TEASPOON SUPERFINE (CASTER) SUGAR
1 TEASPOON WHITE WINE VINEGAR
7 OZ/200 G SHORT PASTA, SUCH AS PENNE
3 EGGPLANTS (AUBERGINES), THINLY SLICED LENGTHWISE
9 OZ/250 G MOZZARELLA CHEESE, TORN INTO BITE-SIZE PIECES
SALT AND FRESHLY GROUND BLACK PEPPER

This show-off dish does require a little effort, but is more than worth it. Cheesy tomato pasta and soft griddled eggplants (aubergines), all in a pie shape. What's not to love?

- To make the sauce, heat the oil in a large nonstick pan, add the onion, and cook over medium heat for 10 minutes, or until softened and golden. Add the garlic and cook for another 1 minute, then add the anchovy fillets with their oil and cook for 2–3 minutes until melted. Add the tomatoes, chili flakes, oregano, sugar, vinegar, and seasoning, then simmer for 20–25 minutes, or until the sauce is slightly reduced and thickened.
- After about 10 minutes, cook the pasta in a large pan of boiling salted water for 8–10 minutes, or according to the package instructions, until just al dente. Taste to check the seasoning of the sauce, then drain the pasta, add to the sauce, and set aside.
- Preheat the oven to 350°F/180°C/Gas mark 4.
- Put 1 tablespoon oil in a small bowl, season with salt and pepper, and then use it to brush the eggplant (aubergine) slices. Heat a griddle pan or skillet (frying pan) over high heat and cook the eggplant slices for 3–4 minutes on each side until softened and lightly browned.
- To make the pasta pie, lightly brush a 10-inch/25-cm cake pan or ovenproof round or oval dish with oil, then line with the eggplant slices, overlapping them so that no gaps appear, reserving 3–4 slices to cover the top.
- Mix the mozzarella cheese into the tomato pasta, then pile into the dish, finishing with the final eggplant slices. Bake in the hot oven for 20 minutes, or until the sauce is piping hot and bubbling, then remove from the oven, rest for 2–3 minutes, and run a knife around the edge to make sure the sides haven't stuck. Carefully invert the pie onto a plate and serve.

SEAFOOD FIDEUA

SERVES 4
PREPARATION TIME: 10 MINUTES
COOKING TIME: 20–25 MINUTES

FROM THE STORE:
SEAFOOD MIX
LEMON

1 TABLESPOON OLIVE OIL
1 LARGE ONION, SLICED
2 CLOVES GARLIC, FINELY CHOPPED
12 OZ/350 G SPAGHETTI
¼ BOUILLON (STOCK) CUBE MADE UP TO 1 CUP (8 FL OZ/250 ML) BROTH (STOCK) WITH BOILING WATER
1 × 14-OZ/400-G CAN CHOPPED TOMATOES
1 TEASPOON CHILI FLAKES
2 TEASPOONS SMOKED PAPRIKA
1 TABLESPOON WHITE WINE VINEGAR
12 OZ/350 G SEAFOOD MIX, DEFROSTED IF FROZEN
1 LEMON, CUT INTO WEDGES, TO SERVE

This classic Spanish dish is similar to paella, but uses short, thin pasta instead. You don't need to find the fideo pasta if you have some spaghetti in the pantry; just snap the spaghetti into ¾ inch/2 cm lengths and it's pretty much the same. Using seafood mix makes this a quick and easy dinner that's reminiscent of sunny days.

- Heat the oil in a large deep skillet (frying pan) or preferably a shallow Dutch oven (casserole dish), add the onion, and cook over medium heat for 5–10 minutes until softened. Add the garlic, cook for another 1 minute, then add the pasta, stirring to coat in the oil. Add the broth (stock), allow the pasta to absorb the water a little, then add the tomatoes, chili flakes, paprika, and vinegar. Reduce the heat to a very gentle simmer and cook for 10–12 minutes until the pasta has absorbed a lot of the liquid and is almost cooked.
- Add the seafood, mix through, then cook for another 5 minutes or until the seafood and pasta are both cooked. Remove from the heat, then serve with lemon wedges.

CAN OF COCONUT MILK

COCONUT ICE CREAM (BASIC RECIPE)

SERVES 6
PREPARATION TIME: 5 MINUTES, PLUS
6–8 HOURS FREEZING

FROM THE STORE:
CONDENSED MILK

1 × 14-OZ/400-G CAN COCONUT MILK
1 × 14-OZ/397-G CAN CONDENSED MILK

The simplest ice cream you will ever make—just one quick stir and you're there. Use this as a base for your favorite flavors.

- Mix both milks together in a large bowl, add your chosen flavorings, then pour into a freezerproof container and freeze for 1 hour. Remove from the freezer, stir, then return to the freezer for another 6–7 hours, or until solid. Remove from the freezer 10 minutes before serving. Alternatively, if you have an ice-cream machine, churn according to the manufacturer's directions until set.

STRAWBERRY AND COCONUT ICE CREAM

FROM THE STORE:
CONDENSED MILK
STRAWBERRIES

1 × COCONUT ICE CREAM (BASIC RECIPE) INGREDIENTS
1¾ CUPS (9 OZ/250 G) STRAWBERRIES, HULLED AND CHOPPED

- Put the strawberries into a bowl and, using a handheld blender, blend to a puree.
- Stir the puree into the coconut and condensed milk mixture and freeze as described in the basic recipe above.

MANGO AND COCONUT ICE CREAM

'ROM THE STORE:
:ONDENSED MILK
:ANNED MANGOES

× COCONUT ICE CREAM (BASIC RECIPE) INGREDIENTS
× 15-OZ/425-G CAN MANGOES, DRAINED

This ice cream is a little softer than the usual custard-based type.

- Put the mango into a bowl and, using a handheld blender, blend to a puree.
- Stir the puree into the coconut and condensed milk mixture and freeze as described in the basic recipe opposite.

 +

VIETNAMESE COFFEE AND COCONUT ICE CREAM

'ROM THE STORE:
:ONDENSED MILK
:ROUND ESPRESSO

× COCONUT ICE CREAM (BASIC RECIPE) INGREDIENTS
;HOT OF ESPRESSO, COOLED

- Stir the espresso shot into the coconut and condensed milk mixture and freeze as described in the basic recipe opposite.

 +

RED LENTIL DHAL WITH CUMIN-ROASTED CAULIFLOWER AND CRISPY LEAVES

SERVES 4
PREPARATION TIME: 15 MINUTES
COOKING TIME: 30 MINUTES

FROM THE STORE:
RED LENTILS
CAULIFLOWER

2 TABLESPOONS OLIVE OIL, PLUS EXTRA FOR OILING
2 ONIONS, FINELY CHOPPED
3 CLOVES GARLIC, FINELY CHOPPED
1 TEASPOON GROUND CUMIN SEEDS
2 TEASPOONS GROUND TURMERIC
1 TEASPOON CHILI FLAKES
1½ CUPS (11 OZ/300 G) RED LENTILS
1 × 14-OZ/400-G CAN COCONUT MILK
1 BOUILLON (STOCK) CUBE MADE UP TO 1½ CUPS (12 FL OZ/350 ML) BROTH (STOCK) WITH BOILING WATER
SALT AND FRESHLY GROUND BLACK PEPPER

FOR THE CUMIN-ROASTED CAULIFLOWER
1 CAULIFLOWER, BROKEN INTO FLORETS, LEAVES SET ASIDE
OLIVE OIL, FOR DRIZZLING
2 TEASPOONS CUMIN SEEDS

TIP:
ANY LEFTOVER DHAL GOES WELL IN A SOURDOUGH SANDWICH WITH A LITTLE GRATED CARROT.

This dhal recipe is a must-have in the repertoire for when you're feeling lazy and need something nutritious. The roasted spiced cauliflower, cooked with its leaves, gives the added flavor and texture needed to make it guest-worthy.

- Heat the oil in a large pan, add the onions, and fry over medium heat for 5–10 minutes until the onions are softened and golden. Add the garlic, cook for another 1 minute until fragrant, then add the spices. Cook for 2 minutes, season, then add the red lentils, stirring until coated in the oil. Add the coconut milk and broth (stock), then bring to a simmer and cook for 20 minutes, or until the lentils have broken down and the liquid has all been absorbed.
- Meanwhile, preheat the broiler (grill) to high and prepare the cumin-roasted cauliflower. Bring a large pan of water to a simmer, add the cauliflower, and cook for 5 minutes until slightly tender. Drain and put on a baking sheet with the leaves. Drizzle with oil and season, then sprinkle over the cumin seeds. Shake the baking sheet until the cauliflower is evenly coated, then broil (grill) the cauliflower for 10 minutes, or until golden brown and beginning to become dark in places. Keep an eye on the leaves. If they look like they are browning too quickly remove them and set aside.
- To serve, check the seasoning of the dhal. You might have to add a splash of water to loosen it a bit as it will set as it sits. Spoon the dhal into bowls and top with the cauliflower florets and leaves.

BANH XEO WITH CRUNCHY CABBAGE AND SOY AND CHILI SHRIMP

SERVES 4–6
PREPARATION TIME: 15 MINUTES, PLUS 20 MINUTES RESTING
COOKING TIME: 15 MINUTES

FROM THE STORE:

UNCOOKED JUMBO SHRIMP (KING PRAWNS)
WHITE CABBAGE

FOR THE PANCAKES
GENEROUS 2 CUPS (9 OZ/250 G) ALL-PURPOSE (PLAIN) FLOUR
½ TEASPOON BAKING POWDER
1 TEASPOON SALT
2½ TEASPOONS GROUND TURMERIC
1 × 14-OZ/400-G CAN COCONUT MILK
SCANT ½ CUP (3½ FL OZ/100 ML) WATER
OLIVE OIL, FOR FRYING

FOR THE FILLING
12 OZ/350 G UNCOOKED JUMBO SHRIMP (KING PRAWNS), PEELED
1½ TABLESPOONS SOY SAUCE, PLUS A LITTLE EXTRA
1 TEASPOON CHILI FLAKES
1 CLOVE GARLIC, FINELY CHOPPED
½ WHITE CABBAGE, FINELY SHREDDED

TIP:
IF YOU HAVE ANY OF THE PORK SIDE (BELLY) LEFT OVER (SEE PAGE 57), TRY SHREDDING THAT AND ADD IT TO THE SOY AND SHRIMP (PRAWN) FILLING.

These Vietnamese pancakes are crisp, filling, and delicious, especially when stuffed with shrimp (prawns) and crunchy cabbage. You can easily make this gluten free by using rice flour instead of all-purpose (plain) flour.

- To make the pancake batter, whisk all the ingredients together in a large bowl to a smooth batter. Set aside for 20 minutes to rest. It should be the consistency of thick, heavy cream.
- Now make the filling. Heat 1 tablespoon oil in a skillet (frying pan), add the shrimp (prawns), and cook over medium heat for about 2 minutes on each side until they start to turn pink. Add the soy sauce, chili flakes, and garlic and cook for another 2 minutes. Remove from the skillet, set aside, and keep warm while you make the pancakes.
- Add a drizzle more oil to the skillet, then pour in a thin layer of batter and swirl around for even coverage. When bubbling on the surface and crisping nicely on the bottom, slide the pancake out of the skillet onto a plate and keep warm. Repeat until all the batter has been used.
- Stuff each pancake with some of the shrimp mixture, a handful of the cabbage, and a dash of soy sauce, then fold one half of the pancake over the top of the filling. These are best served straightaway, but if you like, you can cook the pancakes in advance, keep warm in a low oven, then fill with the shrimp and cabbage once cooked.

COCONUT CHICKEN SOUP

SERVES 2
PREPARATION TIME: 15 MINUTES
COOKING TIME: 15 MINUTES

FROM THE STORE:
CILANTRO (CORIANDER)
BONELESS CHICKEN THIGHS

3½ OZ/100 G LONG PASTA, SUCH AS SPAGHETTI
1 TEASPOON CHILI FLAKES
2 CLOVES GARLIC
1 TABLESPOON WHITE WINE VINEGAR
2 ANCHOVY FILLETS, COARSELY CHOPPED
2 TEASPOONS GROUND TURMERIC
1 BUNCH CILANTRO (CORIANDER), STEMS AND LEAVES FINELY CHOPPED
1 TABLESPOON OLIVE OIL
1 × 14-OZ/400-G CAN COCONUT MILK
1 TABLESPOON SOY SAUCE
1 TEASPOON SUPERFINE (CASTER) SUGAR
4 SKINLESS, BONELESS CHICKEN THIGHS, SLICED

TIP:
DOUBLE THE QUANTITY OF SPICE PASTE AND KEEP IN THE REFRIGERATOR UNDER A THIN LAYER OF OIL FOR NEXT TIME YOU FANCY A TASTY SOUP. THIS WILL KEEP FOR UP TO 1 WEEK.

This recipe is for those times that you really fancy something warming, spicy, and Southeast Asian inspired but you don't have the hundred and one ingredients that usually make up the dish. Try it, we think you will like it, and you can refine it as you go, using different vegetables and flavorings like fresh lime if you like.

- Cook the pasta in a pan of boiling water according to the package directions, until just tender. Drain and refresh under cold water to stop the pasta cooking then set aside.
- Put the chili flakes, garlic, vinegar, anchovies, turmeric, cilantro (coriander) stems, and oil into a food processor and process to a paste. If you don't have a food processor put the dry ingredients on a cutting (chopping) board and run a sharp knife over the lot until really finely chopped. Scrape into a bowl and mix with the vinegar and oil.
- Put a pan over medium heat, scrape the spice paste into the pan, and fry for 1–2 minutes until fragrant. Pour in the coconut milk, soy sauce, and sugar. Add the chicken and cook for about 5 minutes, or until the chicken is piping hot and cooked through. Taste the soup and add a little more sugar or vinegar if it needs a bit of zing. Tip the pasta into the soup and cook for a few minutes to heat through.
- Stir through the cilantro leaves, ladle into big bowls, and serve.

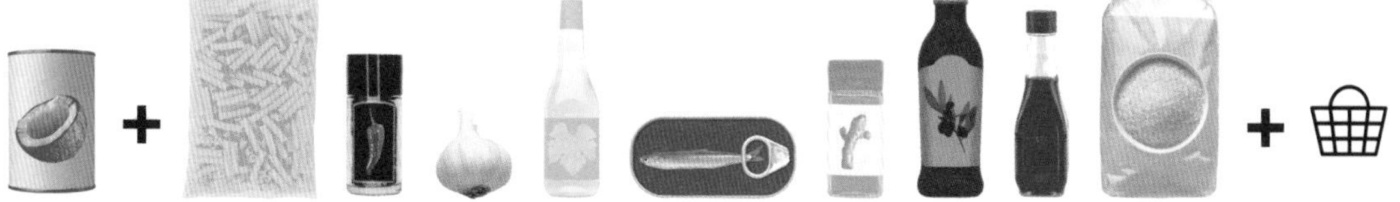

RICE AND PEAS WITH SPICED PORK LOIN STEAKS

SERVES 4
PREPARATION TIME: 15 MINUTES, PLUS 10 MINUTES MARINATING
COOKING TIME: 15 MINUTES, PLUS 5 MINUTES RESTING

FROM THE STORE:
RED KIDNEY BEANS
BONELESS PORK LOIN STEAKS

2 BONELESS PORK LOIN STEAKS
2 TABLESPOONS OLIVE OIL
1 ONION, FINELY CHOPPED
2 CLOVES GARLIC, CHOPPED
1 CUP (7 OZ/200 G) WHITE BASMATI RICE, RINSED
1 × 14-OZ/400-G CAN COCONUT MILK
1 TEASPOON DRIED THYME
1 × 14-OZ/400-G CAN RED KIDNEY BEANS, DRAINED AND RINSED
SALT AND FRESHLY GROUND BLACK PEPPER

FOR THE MARINADE
1 TEASPOON DRIED THYME
2 CLOVES GARLIC, CRUSHED
1 TEASPOON CHILI FLAKES
1 TEASPOON GROUND CINNAMON
1 TEASPOON CUMIN SEEDS, BASHED
1 TABLESPOON SUPERFINE (CASTER) SUGAR
2 TABLESPOONS SOY SAUCE

TIP:
YOU CAN LEAVE THE PORK IN THE MARINADE IN THE REFRIGERATOR ALL DAY WHILE YOU ARE AT WORK, THE FLAVOR WILL HAVE PLENTY OF TIME TO GET INTO THE MEAT.

We use traditional kidney beans in our rice and peas but you can use any beans that are available to you. A bigger bean works best as its creamy texture adds another dimension to the comforting nature of the finished dish.

- For the marinade, put all of the ingredients into a shallow dish and stir to combine and dissolve the sugar.
- Sit the pork in the dish and rub with the marinade. Cover with plastic wrap (clingfilm) and leave for at least 10 minutes.
- Meanwhile, heat 1 tablespoon oil in a large pan, add the onion, and cook over high heat for 2 minutes until starting to soften. Add the garlic and cook for another 30 seconds—you do not want to get any color on the onion and garlic. Add the rice and coconut milk. Pour scant 1 cup (7 fl oz/200 ml) water into the empty can and swirl to remove any coconut milk, then add this to the pan with the thyme. Bring to a boil, reduce the heat, and cook, covered, for 10 minutes.
- When the rice is tender, fluff with a fork then gently fold through the kidney beans with plenty of salt and pepper. Remove from the heat and let stand for 5 minutes.
- Meanwhile, heat the remaining oil in a large nonstick skillet (frying pan). Lift the pork out of the marinade, wipe off any excess, then fry over high heat for 2–3 minutes on each side, depending on how thick your steaks are. Transfer the pork to a plate and rest, covered with aluminum foil, for 5 minutes. Put the skillet back on the heat and tip in the marinade with 2 tablespoons water, swirl the pan to collect any meat juices, and boil for 1 minute.
- Thinly slice the pork and serve with the rice and peas and any pan juices.

COCONUT MILK PANNA COTTA WITH CARAMELIZED PINEAPPLE

SERVES 4
PREPARATION TIME: 10 MINUTES, PLUS 4 HOURS SETTING
COOKING TIME: 10 MINUTES, PLUS COOLING

FROM THE STORE:

GELATIN LEAVES OR POWDERED GELATIN
PINEAPPLE

3 GELATIN LEAVES, CUT INTO PIECES, OR 2 TEASPOONS POWDERED GELATIN
OLIVE OIL, FOR OILING
1 × 14-OZ/400-G CAN COCONUT MILK
GENEROUS ⅓ CUP (2¾ OZ/75 G) SUPERFINE (CASTER) SUGAR, PLUS 2 TEASPOONS FOR THE PINEAPPLE
½ PINEAPPLE, PEELED, CORED, AND CUT INTO 4 RINGS

TIP:
YOU CAN REPLACE THE PINEAPPLE WITH ANY FRESH, SEASONAL FRUIT, OR EVEN TOASTED COCONUT FLAKES, IF YOU LIKE.

This dessert is a winner for those with dairy intolerances, and even for those without. It is especially good served after a hot curry or the Pork Side with Egg Fried Rice and Sticky Dipping Sauce on page 57.

- Put the gelatin leaves into a bowl of cold water and soak for 5 minutes until softened. Alternatively, if using powdered gelatin, put 2 tablespoons water into a small saucepan and sprinkle over the gelatin. Let stand for 5 minutes until the gelatin has become hydrated.
- Lightly oil 4 ramekins.
- Put the coconut milk into a pan with the sugar, and heat over low heat until just before it reaches a simmer. Drain the gelatin, and squeeze out as much excess water as possible. Remove the coconut milk from the heat and whisk in the gelatin until it is completely dissolved. If using powdered gelatin, place the saucepan over a low heat to melt the gelatin. Heat until steaming, but do not boil. Pour the warm coconut milk into the pan and stir well.
- Transfer the coconut milk mixture to a bowl set in a roasting pan half filled with ice water. Stir every few minutes until the mixture thickens to the consistency of Greek yogurt.
- Pour the thickened coconut milk mixture into the prepared ramekins and cool to room temperature, then chill in the refrigerator for 4 hours, or until set.
- To serve, preheat the broiler (grill) to high. Run a knife gently around the edge of the ramekins, then dip the bottoms into a bowl of warm water and quickly invert onto a plate.
- Sprinkle the pineapple rings with the remaining sugar, then cook under the hot broiler for 2–3 minutes, or until browned. Chop the pineapple rings into pieces and use to decorate the panna cottas.

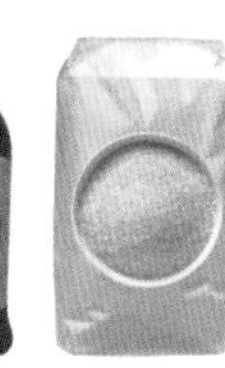

COCONUT AND LIME MERINGUE PIE

SERVES 8–10
PREPARATION TIME: 10 MINUTES, PLUS 20 MINUTES CHILLING
COOKING TIME: 1 HOUR, PLUS COOLING

FROM THE STORE:

SWEET BASIC PIE DOUGH (SHORTCRUST PASTRY)
LIMES

- 13¼-OZ/375-G STORE-BOUGHT SWEET BASIC PIE DOUGH (SHORTCRUST PASTRY), DEFROSTED IF FROZEN
- 1 × 14-OZ/400-G CAN COCONUT MILK
- GENEROUS ⅓ CUP (2¾ OZ/75 G) SUPERFINE (CASTER) SUGAR, PLUS 2 TABLESPOONS FOR THE MERINGUE
- 3 TABLESPOONS ALL-PURPOSE (PLAIN) FLOUR
- 3 EGGS, YOLKS AND WHITES SEPARATED
- 1 WHOLE EGG
- ZEST AND JUICE OF 2 LIMES

This pie is creamy with a zip of lime—it is like a more indulgent-tasting version of a lemon meringue pie.

- Roll out the pastry on a lightly floured work counter and use to line an 8-inch/20-cm tart pan, loose-bottomed cake pan, or a pie dish—all will work well. Place the pie crust (pastry case) on a flat baking sheet and transfer to the fridge to chill for about 20 minutes.
- Preheat the oven to 350°F/180°C/Gas mark 4.
- Remove the pie crust from the refrigerator, scrunch up a large piece of parchment (baking) paper, and use it to line the pie crust. Fill with pie weights or baking beans and blind bake in the hot oven for 15 minutes. Remove the paper and weights or beans, return the pie crust to the oven and cook for another 5–10 minutes, until pale golden. Place on a wire rack and let cool while you make the filling.
- Pour the coconut milk into a small pan and whisk in the sugar and flour. Heat the mixture very gently over a low heat until hot and thickened. Be careful not to let the coconut milk boil otherwise it may split.
- Place the egg yolks and whole egg in a bowl then slowly pour on the hot coconut milk mixture while stirring. Pass the mixture through a sieve into a clean bowl to remove any eggy threads. Stir in the lime juice and zest.
- Reduce the oven temperature to 325°F/160°C/Gas mark 3. Place the pie crust on a lipped baking sheet then carefully pour the coconut custard into the tart base. Bake for 30–35 minutes, or until just set.
- Allow the tart to cool completely—at this point you can chill the tart until ready to serve. Once the tart has cooled, preheat the broiler (grill) to high.
- Just before you are ready to serve, beat the egg whites to stiff peaks in a bowl with an electric whisk. Once stiff, gradually add the remaining sugar a little at a time, whisking well after each addition to make sure the sugar has dissolved. The meringue is ready when it is thick and glossy. Dollop the meringue over the top of the cooled custard and swirl with the back of a spoon to coat the surface. Place under the hot broiler for 1–2 minutes until a pale golden color. Serve.

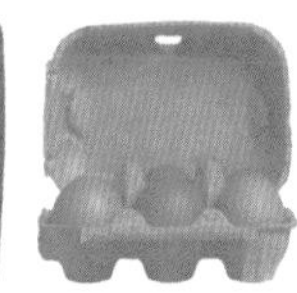

OUR TRES LECHES CAKE

SERVES 8–10
PREPARATION TIME: 15 MINUTES, PLUS 1 HOUR CHILLING
COOKING TIME: 25–30 MINUTES

FROM THE STORE:
SWEETENED CONDENSED MILK
HEAVY (DOUBLE) CREAM

OLIVE OIL, FOR OILING
3 EGGS
¾ CUP (5 OZ/150 G) SUPERFINE (CASTER) SUGAR
1¼ CUPS (5 OZ/150 G) ALL-PURPOSE (PLAIN) FLOUR
1 TEASPOON BAKING POWDER
½ TEASPOON GROUND CINNAMON, PLUS EXTRA FOR DUSTING

FOR THE FILLING
1 × 14-OZ/397-G CAN SWEETENED CONDENSED MILK
½ × 14-OZ/400-G CAN COCONUT MILK
1¼ CUPS (10 FL OZ/300 ML) HEAVY (DOUBLE) CREAM

TIP:
THIS CAKE IS BEST EATEN ON THE DAY IT IS MADE.

Usually the lightly whisked sponge that is the base for Mexican tres leches cake is soaked in a mixture of condensed and evaporated milks and heavy (double) cream. Here, we have swapped the evaporated milk for rich coconut milk, which tastes lighter and less sweet than the traditional mix but is still just as delicious.

- Preheat the oven to 350°F/180°C/Gas mark 4 and oil and line an 8-inch/20-cm round springform cake pan with parchment (baking) paper.
- Beat the eggs and sugar together in a large bowl with an electric whisk until the mixture is pale, creamy, and almost trebled in volume. This will take about 8 minutes, so be patient.
- Sift the flour, baking powder, and cinnamon over the egg mixture. Gently but efficiently fold the flour into the mix using a metal spoon. Make sure you dig right down to the bottom of the bowl to reach all of the flour. It is important to keep as much air as possible in the batter at this stage. Scrape the cake batter into the prepared pan and bake in the hot oven for 25–30 minutes until the cake is golden, risen, and a skewer inserted into the center comes out clean.
- Meanwhile, in a large bowl, mix the condensed milk, coconut milk, and half the heavy (double) cream together until smooth, then set aside.
- Remove the cake from the oven and place on a baking sheet. Use a toothpick to make small holes all over the surface of the cake right down to the bottom. Pour over half of the milk mixture and let it soak in. Pour over the remaining milk mixture, transfer to the refrigerator, and chill for at least an hour to let the sponge absorb all of the creamy milk filling.
- Before you are ready to serve, unmold the cake, leaving the bottom of the pan intact, and place on a serving plate. The final texture should be quite squidgy.
- Lightly whip the remaining heavy cream to soft peaks. Spread the cream over the surface of the cake and dust lightly with cinnamon. Slice into wedges and serve with a strong coffee.

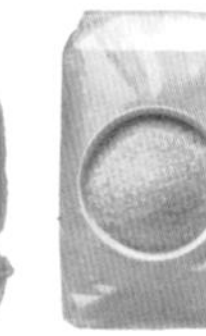

BAR OF CHOCOLATE

CHOCOLATE GANACHE (BASIC RECIPE)

SERVES 6
PREPARATION TIME: 5 MINUTES
COOKING TIME: 5 MINUTES

FROM THE STORE:
HEAVY (DOUBLE) CREAM

7 OZ/200 G BITTERSWEET (DARK) CHOCOLATE, FINELY CHOPPED
1¼ CUPS (10 FL OZ/300 ML) HEAVY (DOUBLE) CREAM

This simple chocolate sauce is honestly the most foolproof recipe ever, so be bold and turn it into one of the following more show-off desserts.

- Put the chocolate into a heatproof bowl, then heat the cream in a small pan over low heat until almost boiling, and pour over the chopped chocolate. Let stand for about 2 minutes, then stir until smooth.

 + 

CLASSIC CHOCOLATE TART

FROM THE STORE:
HEAVY (DOUBLE) CREAM
READY-ROLLED SWEET BASIC PIE DOUGH (SHORTCRUST) PASTRY

11¼ OZ/320 G READY-ROLLED SWEET BASIC PIE DOUGH (SHORTCRUST PASTRY)
1 × QUANTITY CHOCOLATE GANACHE (BASIC RECIPE)

- Preheat the oven to 350°F/180°C/Gas mark 4. Line an 8-inch/20-cm fluted tart pan with the sweet pie dough (shortcrust pastry), then line with parchment (baking) paper and add pie weights or baking beans. Bake in the hot oven for 15 minutes. Remove the parchment paper and weights or beans, return the pie crust (pastry case)to the oven and bake for another 10 minutes until golden and crispy. Place on a wire rack and cool, then fill with the ganache and let set in the refrigerator for at least 30 minutes.

 + 

CHOCOLATE AND HAZELNUT TRUFFLES

FROM THE STORE:
HEAVY (DOUBLE) CREAM
HAZELNUTS

1 × QUANTITY CHOCOLATE GANACHE (BASIC RECIPE)
⅔ CUP (5 OZ/150 G) CHOPPED TOASTED HAZELNUTS

- Let the ganache cool until thickened and stiff—it's best left in the refrigerator to firm up—then scoop out balls with a teaspoon or melon baller dipped in hot water. Drop the balls into the hazelnuts and roll to coat. You should end up with about 20 or so truffles.
- Serve immediately or store in an airtight container in the refrigerator until ready to serve.

ROSEMARY CHOCOLATE POTS

FROM THE STORE:
HEAVY (DOUBLE) CREAM
ROSEMARY

1 × CHOCOLATE GANACHE (BASIC RECIPE) INGREDIENTS
2 TABLESPOONS FINELY CHOPPED ROSEMARY

- Follow the basic recipe for chocolate ganache (opposite), adding the rosemary (reserving about 1 teaspoon to serve) to the cream before heating. Pour the rosemary cream over the chopped chocolate. Let stand for about 2 minutes, then stir until smooth.
- Pour the ganache into 6 small glasses, tea cups, or ramekins, then chill for 20 minutes until set.
- Top the chilled pots with the reserved rosemary and serve.

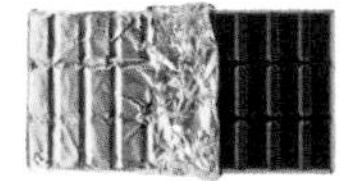

CHUNKY BEEF CHILI WITH RICE

SERVES 4–6
PREPARATION TIME: 15 MINUTES
COOKING TIME: 2½ HOURS

FROM THE STORE:
STEWING STEAK
CILANTRO (CORIANDER)

2 TABLESPOONS OLIVE OIL
1 LB 2 OZ/500 G STEWING STEAK, CUT INTO LARGE CUBES
2 ONIONS, THINLY SLICED
2 CLOVES GARLIC, CHOPPED
1 TABLESPOON SMOKED PAPRIKA
2 TEASPOONS CUMIN SEEDS, BASHED
1 TEASPOON CHILI FLAKES
1 TEASPOON GROUND CINNAMON
1 × 14-OZ/400-G CAN CHOPPED TOMATOES
1 × 14-OZ/400-G CAN CHICKPEAS, DRAINED AND RINSED
1 BOUILLON (STOCK) CUBE
1 BUNCH CILANTRO (CORIANDER), STEMS AND LEAVES CHOPPED
2¾ OZ/75 G BITTERSWEET (DARK) CHOCOLATE, CHOPPED
SALT AND FRESHLY GROUND BLACK PEPPER
FRESHLY COOKED RICE, TO SERVE

TIP:
THIS IS A NIGH-ON PERFECT FREEZER DINNER. YOU'LL BE GRATEFUL FOR IT ON A DEPRESSING AND RAINY MONDAY NIGHT OR A HUNGOVER SUNDAY.

We are using our trusty can of chickpeas in our chili recipe. If, however, you are a traditionalist grab yourself a 14-oz/400-g can of kidney beans and add these into the mix instead.

- Heat half the oil in a Dutch oven (casserole dish) or large high-sided skillet (frying pan) with a lid, add the steak, and cook over medium heat for 5–10 minutes until the steak is browned all over—you may have to do this in batches. Remove from the skillet and set aside.
- Add the remaining oil to the skillet, then add the onions and cook for 5 minutes, or until soft and starting to take on some color. Add the garlic, paprika, cumin, chili flakes, and cinnamon and fry for another 1 minute. Return the chunks of steak along with any resting juices to the skillet. Add the tomatoes and chickpeas, then put the bouillon (stock) cube into the empty tomato can and fill to the top with boiling water, stir to dissolve the bouillon cube, and add this to the skillet along with the cilantro (coriander) stems. Bring to a boil, then reduce the heat, cover with a lid, and simmer gently for 2 hours, or until the beef is really tender—if the chili looks like it is drying out add a splash of water.
- When the cooking time is up, uncover and stir in the chocolate. Add plenty of seasoning and cook for another 5 minutes, or until the sauce is thick and the chocolate has melted.
- Serve the chili sprinkled with cilantro and freshly cooked rice.

CHOCOLATE AND PISTACHIO BISCOTTI

MAKES 14–16
PREPARATION TIME: 15 MINUTES
COOKING TIME: 1 HOUR, PLUS COOLING

FROM THE STORE:
UNSALTED SHELLED PISTACHIOS

⅔ CUP (3½ OZ/100 G) UNSALTED SHELLED PISTACHIOS
1 CUP (4½ OZ/125 G) ALL-PURPOSE (PLAIN) FLOUR
1 TEASPOON BAKING POWDER
PINCH OF SALT
GENEROUS ⅓ CUP (2¾ OZ/75 G) SUPERFINE (CASTER) SUGAR
1 EGG, BEATEN
1 TABLESPOON MILK
2¾ OZ/75 G BITTERSWEET (DARK) CHOCOLATE, COARSELY CHOPPED

TIP:
THESE WILL KEEP IN A CONTAINER FOR A GOOD WEEK OR TWO.

This recipe is one from the archives of our dear friend Dave, who can testify that it is a simple crowd pleaser. Once you have mastered it, you can mix and match the ingredients as you like. White chocolate and apricot, date and walnut, and fig and cranberry all work wonderfully.

- Preheat the oven to 340°F/170°C/Gas mark 4 and line a baking sheet with parchment (baking) paper.
- Measure out half the pistachios and process in a food processor until finely ground. Alternatively, finely chop the pistachios, then grind in a mortar with a pestle until fine. Very coarsely chop the remaining pistachios.
- In a large bowl, thoroughly mix the flour, baking powder, salt, sugar, and ground pistachios together. Mix in the egg and milk, then add the chopped pistachios and chocolate. Mix to a dough, then shape into a log, 2–2½ inches/5–6 cm in width.
- Put the log onto the prepared baking sheet and bake in the hot oven for about 30 minutes until golden. Cool on the sheet for 10 minutes, then transfer to a wire rack to cool completely.
- Reduce the oven temperature to 300°F/150°C/Gas mark 2 and line another baking sheet with parchment paper.
- Using a serrated knife, cut the cooled log into diagonal slices, about ½ inch/1 cm wide and put on the prepared baking sheet. Return to the oven for another 30 minutes, turning over half way through, or until crisp. Cool on a wire rack, then store in an airtight container.

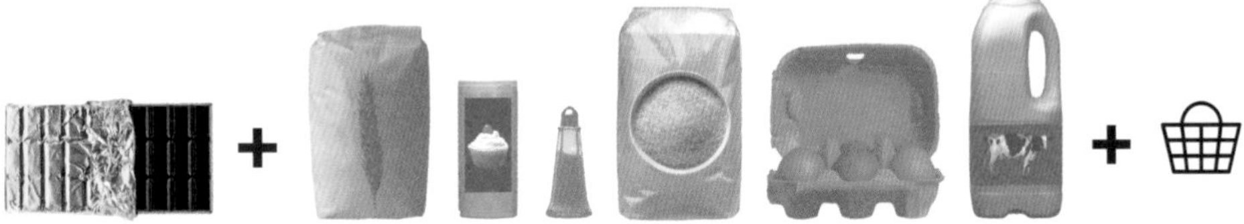

CHOCOLATE, CHERRY, AND COCONUT SHEET CAKE

MAKES 12 SQUARES
PREPARATION TIME: 5 MINUTES
COOKING TIME: 20 MINUTES, PLUS COOLING

FROM THE STORE:

DRY UNSWEETENED (DESICCATED) COCONUT
SOUR CHERRIES

- 2 EGGS, LIGHTLY BEATEN
- ½ CUP (3½ OZ/100 G) SUPERFINE (CASTER) SUGAR
- 2½ CUPS (7 OZ/200 G) DRY UNSWEETENED (DESICCATED) COCONUT
- 7 OZ/200 G BITTERSWEET (DARK) CHOCOLATE, COARSELY CHOPPED
- GENEROUS ½ CUP (3½ OZ/100 G) SOUR CHERRIES, COARSELY CHOPPED

TIP:
THIS MIXTURE CAN BE MADE INTO INDIVIDUAL COOKIES IF YOU PREFER. SIMPLY SPOON TABLESPOONSFUL ONTO PREPARED BAKING SHEETS AND COOK IN THE HOT OVEN FOR 12 MINUTES, OR UNTIL LIGHT GOLDEN AND SET. COOL COMPLETELY ON THE BAKING SHEETS.

A mixture of any dried fruit will work in this sheet cake (traybake), just keep the ratios the same and you will have a great teatime treat.

- Preheat the oven to 350°F/180°C/Gas mark 4 and line an 8 × 12-inch/20 × 30-cm baking sheet with parchment (baking) paper.
- Mix the eggs, sugar, and coconut in a bowl until combined, add the chocolate and sour cherries, and stir to combine. Scrape the mixture onto the prepared sheet and spread out to an even layer. Bake in the oven for 20 minutes, or until lightly golden and set. Remove from the hot oven and cool completely. Use a serrated knife to cut the sheet cake (traybake) into squares.

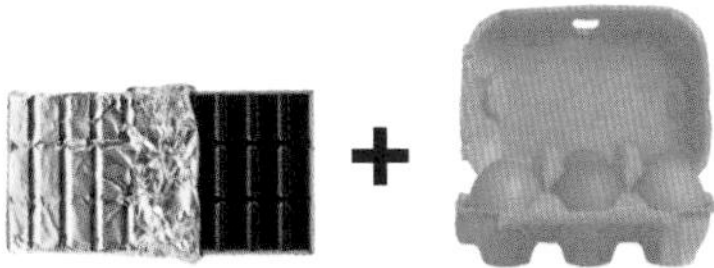  + 

OLIVE OIL AND SEA SALT CHOCOLATE TOASTIES

SERVES 2
PREPARATION TIME: 5 MINUTES
COOKING TIME: 5 MINUTES

FROM THE STORE:
GOOD-QUALITY CRUSTY BREAD OR WHITE SOURDOUGH

2¾ OZ/75 G MILK OR BITTERSWEET (DARK) CHOCOLATE, BROKEN INTO SQUARES
4 SLICES GOOD-QUALITY CRUSTY BREAD OR WHITE SOURDOUGH
SALT, FOR SPRINKLING
2 TABLESPOONS OLIVE OIL

TIP:
TRY SERVING THIS WITH FRESH ORANGE SEGMENTS ON THE SIDE.

This is a riff on a classic Spanish dessert, where chocolate ganache is souped up with a drizzle of olive oil and a sprinkling of flaky sea salt. It makes for a pretty decent snack and even better breakfast. Just eat an apple afterwards if you feel guilty.

- Divide the chocolate pieces between 2 slices of bread, sprinkle with salt, then sandwich with the remaining 2 slices of bread.
- Put a skillet (frying pan) big enough to fit both sandwiches over medium heat, then brush the top of the sandwiches liberally with olive oil. Put the sandwiches, in the pan, oil-side down, and fry for about 2–3 minutes until golden.
- Brush the unoiled bread with oil then flip the sandwich over and fry again for another 2 minutes, or until the chocolate is oozing, then serve immediately.

TOASTED MARSHMALLOW, CHOCOLATE, AND RASPBERRY TEACAKES

MAKES 9
PREPARATION TIME: 10 MINUTES
COOKING TIME: 15 MINUTES, PLUS COOLING

FROM THE STORE:
MARSHMALLOWS
RASPBERRIES

OLIVE OIL, FOR OILING
7 OZ/200 G BITTERSWEET (DARK) CHOCOLATE, COARSELY CHOPPED
1 EGG
¼ CUP (2 OZ/50 G) SUPERFINE (CASTER) SUGAR
½ CUP PLUS 2 TABLESPOONS (2¾ OZ/75 G) ALL-PURPOSE (PLAIN) FLOUR
½ TEASPOON BAKING POWDER
3 CUPS (5 OZ/150 G) MARSHMALLOWS
27 RASPBERRIES

TIP:
USE FRESH OR FROZEN RASPBERRIES DEPENDING ON THE SEASON. DURING THE WINTER MONTHS WHEN FRESH BERRIES ARE DIFFICULT TO GET HOLD OF THEIR FROZEN COUNTERPARTS WILL BE SWEETER.

This is the grown-up version of a childhood favorite. The fresh raspberry cuts through the sweetness of the marshmallow, making it taste more like a dessert than a sweet snack.

- Preheat the oven to 400°F/200°C/Gas mark 6 and oil a 12-section muffin pan. Cut out 9 small circles of parchment (baking) paper and push these into the bottom of 9 sections.
- Put the chocolate into a microwavable bowl and microwave in 20-second intervals, stirring after each one, until the chocolate is melted and smooth. Cool. Alternatively, put the chocolate in a heatproof bowl set over a pan of gently simmering water, making sure the bottom of the bowl doesn't touch the water, and leave until melted. Remove from the heat and stir until smooth then cool.
- Whisk the egg and sugar together in a large bowl until really pale and almost doubled in volume. Fold in three-quarters of the cooled chocolate then sift over the flour and baking powder and fold in until thoroughly combined.
- Divide the batter among the 9 lined muffin sections—don't worry if you don't think you have enough batter, there will only be about a heaping tablespoon in each section. Bake in the hot oven for 5 minutes, or until risen and springy to the touch. Cool in the pan.
- Meanwhile, put the marshmallows in a large heatproof bowl set over a pan of boiling water, making sure the bottom of the bowl doesn't touch the water. Add 1 tablespoon boiling water and stir constantly until the marshmallows have melted into a sticky mess. Remove from the heat.
- Preheat the broiler (grill) to high. Unmold the cakes and put on a baking sheet. Put a little dollop of marshmallow in the middle of each cake then dot 3 raspberries on top. Use 2 teaspoons to cover the raspberries with plenty of the marshmallow then flash the topped cakes under the broiler for about 30 seconds or until the marshmallows are lightly toasted. You can also use a blowtorch set on a gentle heat if you have one. Remove from the heat and cool.
- Drizzle the remaining melted chocolate over the teacakes and allow to set before eating. If your chocolate has set, pop it back over a pan of boiling water to melt.

 + 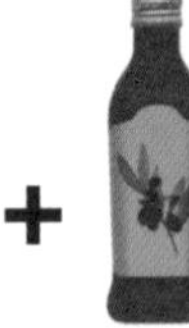 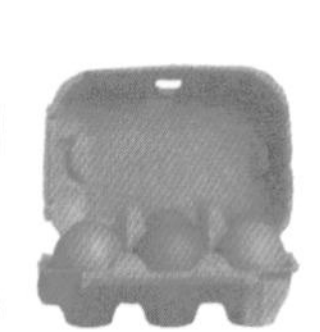  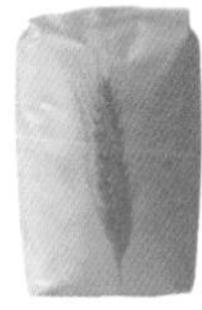  + 

SALTED CARAMEL MILLIONAIRE'S SHORTBREAD

MAKES 16 SQUARES
PREPARATION TIME: 15 MINUTES
COOKING TIME: 45 MINUTES, PLUS COOLING

FROM THE STORE:

BUTTER
CONDENSED MILK

1½ CUPS (6½ OZ/185 G) ALL-PURPOSE PLAIN FLOUR
1¼ STICKS (5 OZ/150 G) COLD BUTTER, DICED
¼ CUP + 2 TABLESPOONS (2¾ OZ/75 G) SUPERFINE (CASTER) SUGAR
7 OZ/200 G BITTERSWEET (DARK) CHOCOLATE, COARSELY CHOPPED

FOR THE FILLING
5 TABLESPOONS (2¾ OZ/75G) BUTTER
¼ CUP (2 OZ/50 G) SUPERFINE (CASTER) SUGAR
14-OZ/397-G CAN CONDENSED MILK
A PINCH SALT

TIP:
THE SHORTBREAD DOUGH IS DELICIOUS DUSTED WITH EXTRA SUGAR AND SIMPLY BAKED AS A PLAIN COOKIE TO SERVE WITH A CUP OF TEA.

A pinch of salt makes this tooth-ticklingly sweet treat a little more grown-up. It's perfect with a strong cup of coffee.

- Preheat the oven to 300°F/150°C/Gas mark 2 and line an 8-inch/20-cm square cake pan with parchment (baking) paper.
- Put the flour and butter into a large bowl and, using your fingertips, rub the butter into the flour until the mixture resembles fine bread crumbs. Stir in the sugar and bring the mixture loosely together with your hands. Transfer the mixture to the prepared pan and spread out in an even layer, pressing the shortbread with the flat of your hand so it is firmly packed in. Bake in the hot oven for 30 minutes, or until light golden, then remove from the oven and cool.
- To make the filling, put the butter, sugar, condensed milk, and salt into a small pan over medium heat and stir for 2 minutes until the butter is melted and the sugar has dissolved. Once you have reached this point increase the temperature and bring the mixture to a boil—keep stirring until the caramel thickens and turns a rich golden brown color—about 5 minutes. Remove from the heat and cool for about 2 minutes in the pan then pour over the cooled shortbread base. Cool completely.
- Put the chocolate into a microwavable bowl and microwave in 20-second intervals, stirring after each one, until the chocolate is melted and smooth. Alternatively, put the chocolate in a heatproof bowl set over a pan of gently simmering water, making sure the bottom of the bowl doesn't touch the water, and leave until melted. Pour the melted chocolate over the caramel and leave to set completely. Cut into squares and serve.

FLOURLESS CHOCOLATE AND ALMOND CAKE

SERVES 6–8
PREPARATION TIME: 5 MINUTES
COOKING TIME: 45 MINUTES, PLUS COOLING

FROM THE STORE:
GROUND ALMONDS
LIGHT (SINGLE) CREAM

OLIVE OIL, FOR OILING
7 OZ/200 G BITTERSWEET (DARK) CHOCOLATE, COARSELY CHOPPED
4 EGGS, SEPARATED
¾ CUP (5 OZ/150 G) SUPERFINE (CASTER) SUGAR, PLUS 4 TABLESPOONS
2¼ CUPS (7 OZ/200 G) GROUND ALMONDS
LIGHT (SINGLE) CREAM, TO SERVE

TIP:
IF YOU HAVE AN ABUNDANCE OF HALF-EATEN BAGS OF NUTS, GRIND THEM TO A FINE POWDER IN A FOOD PROCESSOR AND USE IN PLACE OF GROUND ALMONDS. JUST MAKE SURE YOU DON'T MAKE NUT BUTTER.

This cake is perfect for anyone who loves a rich chocolate cake but can't eat flour.

- Preheat the oven to 350°F/180°C/Gas mark 4 and oil and line an 8-inch/20-cm springform cake pan with parchment (baking) paper.
- Put 6 oz/175 g of the chocolate into a microwavable bowl and microwave in 20-second intervals until the chocolate is melted and smooth, then cool. Alternatively, put the chocolate in a heatproof bowl set over a pan of gently simmering water, making sure the bottom of the bowl doesn't touch the water, and leave until melted. Remove from the heat and stir until smooth. Let cool.
- Whisk the egg yolks and sugar in a large bowl until pale, creamy, and almost doubled in volume. This will take about 7 minutes so be patient. Gently fold in the melted chocolate followed by the almonds.
- In another bowl, whisk the egg whites to stiff peaks, then gradually add 2 tablespoons sugar and continue to beat until the whites are really stiff and shiny. Use a large metal spoon to fold one-third of the whites into the chocolate mixture—this will loosen the mix. Gradually fold in the remaining egg whites, keeping as much air as possible in the mixture.
- Scrape the mixture into the prepared pan and bake in the hot oven for 35 minutes, or until a crust has formed on the top of the cake and a skewer inserted into the center only has a few crumbs stuck to it.
- Cool for 10 minutes in the pan then remove from the pan and transfer to a wire rack to cool completely.
- Melt the remaining chocolate as before and drizzle over the top of the cake.
- Softly whip the cream with the remaining sugar.
- Serve the cake cut into wedges with the softly whipped cream on the side.

BOTTLE OF MILK

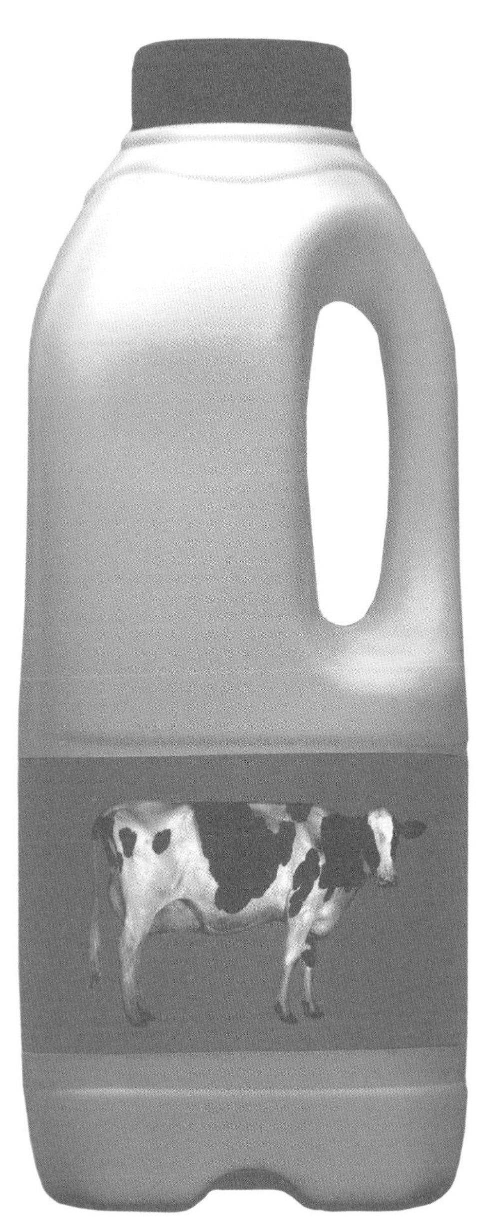

HOMEMADE RICOTTA (BASIC RECIPE)

SERVES 2–4
PREPARATION TIME: 15 MINUTES, PLUS 15 MINUTES STANDING AND 20–30 MINUTES DRAINING
COOKING TIME: 10 MINUTES

6¼ CUPS (50 FL OZ/1.5 LITERS) MILK
2 TABLESPOONS WHITE WINE VINEGAR
½ TEASPOON SALT

This is so much simpler than it sounds, and so much more impressive to friends than you'd think possible.

- Put the milk into a large pan and heat to just before boiling point. Pour in the vinegar, add the salt, then remove from the heat and let stand for 15 minutes. The milk will curdle, and the curds and whey will begin to separate in this time.
- Place a piece of cheesecloth (muslin) in a strainer (sieve) set over a large bowl, then pour the milk mixture into the strainer and let the liquid drain, leaving behind the ricotta. Drain for 20–30 minutes for soft ricotta, but for longer if you like a firmer consistency.

RYE, RICOTTA, AND CHIVE TARTINE

FROM THE STORE:
RYE BREAD
CHIVES

2 SLICES RYE BREAD
1 × QUANTITY HOMEMADE RICOTTA (BASIC RECIPE)
2 TABLESPOONS CHOPPED CHIVES
OLIVE OIL, FOR DRIZZLING
FRESHLY GROUND BLACK PEPPER

- Toast the slices of rye bread.
- Mix the ricotta with the chives, a drizzle of oil, and black pepper in a bowl. Spread on the toast and serve.

RICOTTA, FIG, AND HONEY BOWL

FROM THE STORE:
FIGS
HONEY

1 × QUANTITY HOMEMADE RICOTTA (BASIC RECIPE)
2 FIGS, HALVED
HONEY, FOR DRIZZLING

- Divide the ricotta between 2 dishes, top with the figs then drizzle with honey.

 +   +  

BAKED GARLIC-AND-THYME RICOTTA WITH PITA CHIPS

FROM THE STORE:
PITA BREADS
FRESH THYME

1 × QUANTITY HOMEMADE RICOTTA (BASIC RECIPE)
5 TABLESPOONS OLIVE OIL
½ TEASPOON CHILI FLAKES
1 CLOVE GARLIC, THINLY SLICED
4 PITA BREADS
2 TABLESPOONS THYME LEAVES
1 TEASPOON SMOKED PAPRIKA

- Preheat the oven to 350°F/180°C/Gas mark 4.
- Put the strained ricotta into a small ovenproof dish, then drizzle with 2 tablespoons oil, and sprinkle with the chili flakes and garlic.
- Tear the pita breads into bite-size pieces, put on a baking sheet, and drizzle with the remaining oil. Sprinkle with the thyme and paprika and bake in the hot oven for 10–15 minutes. After 5–10 minutes, stir the pita chips then put the ricotta in the oven for the remaining 5 minutes. Serve immediately.

 +       + 

CHICKEN COOKED IN MILK WITH LEMON AND GARLIC

SERVES 4–6
PREPARATION TIME: 10 MINUTES
COOKING TIME: 1½ HOURS

FROM THE STORE:
WHOLE CHICKEN
LEMONS

1 × 3¼-LB/1.5-KG WHOLE CHICKEN
2 TABLESPOONS OLIVE OIL
1 TEASPOON WHOLE GRAIN MUSTARD
2½ CUPS (20 FL OZ/600 ML) MILK
1 BULB GARLIC, CLOVES PEELED AND LEFT WHOLE
2 LEMONS, ZESTED AND CUT INTO WEDGES
SALT AND FRESHLY GROUND BLACK PEPPER

This is pretty much the simplest and most failsafe one-pot dish you could hope for, inspired by a classic Jamie Oliver recipe. Serve with mash or roast potatoes and some simple greens.

- Preheat the oven to 350°F/180°C/Gas mark 4.
- Season the chicken generously with salt and pepper. Heat the oil in a Dutch oven (casserole dish) large enough to fit the chicken over medium-high heat. Add the chicken and fry for about 5 minutes until the chicken is browned all over.
- In a bowl, whisk the mustard into the milk, then pour into the Dutch oven and add the remaining ingredients. Cover with the lid and cook in the hot oven for 1½ hours, basting 2 or 3 times during cooking. The milk will curdle but don't worry, it's supposed to. When done—insert a skewer into the thickest part of the chicken, such as the thigh, and if the juices that run out are clear it is cooked, if pink then cook for a few minutes longer, and test again.
- When done, cut the bird into pieces and serve drizzled with the sauce and curds.

SAUSAGE AND SAGE TOAD IN THE HOLE WITH GRAVY

SERVES 4
PREPARATION TIME: 15 MINUTES
COOKING TIME: 50 MINUTES

FROM THE STORE:
ITALIAN-STYLE PORK SAUSAGES
SAGE LEAVES

FOR THE TOAD IN THE HOLE
1–2 TABLESPOONS OLIVE OIL
8 ITALIAN-STYLE PORK SAUSAGES
1¼ CUPS (5 OZ/140 G) ALL-PURPOSE (PLAIN) FLOUR
3 EGGS
SCANT 1 CUP (7 FL OZ/200 ML) MILK
10 SAGE LEAVES, SHREDDED
SALT AND FRESHLY GROUND BLACK PEPPER

FOR THE GRAVY
2 TABLESPOONS OLIVE OIL
2 ONIONS, FINELY SLICED
2 TEASPOONS SUPERFINE (CASTER) SUGAR
1 TABLESPOON ALL-PURPOSE (PLAIN) FLOUR
1 TEASPOON SOY SAUCE
¼ BOUILLON (STOCK) CUBE MADE UP TO 1 CUP (8 FL OZ/250 ML) BROTH (STOCK)
SALT AND FRESHLY GROUND BLACK PEPPER

TIP:
YOU CAN ALSO MAKE THIS IN A 12-SECTION MUFFIN PAN IF YOU LIKE—JUST CUT THE SAUSAGES INTO CHUNKS, THEN REDUCE THE COOKING TIME TO 20–25 MINUTES.

This is a British household favorite, a dish of sausages baked in a popover (Yorkshire pudding) batter. It is much easier to make than you'd think. Herby, hot Italian-style sausages work best here, but if you want to make it vegetarian, try replacing them with chunks of squash.

- Preheat the oven to 425°F/220°C/Gas mark 7.
- Put 1 tablespoon oil into a large roasting pan (2 tablespoons if your sausages are not very fatty), add the sausages, turning to coat in the oil, and then cook in the hot oven for 10 minutes, or until browned.
- Meanwhile, make the batter. Put the flour and seasoning into a large bowl, make a well in the center, and pour the eggs into it. Gradually pour in the milk, whisking to a smooth batter, it should be the consistency of heavy (double) cream. Stir through the shredded sage.
- Remove the pan from the oven, then, working quickly, pour the batter evenly into the pan and return to the oven. The key to a puffy Yorkshire pudding is not to open the oven door, so resist the temptation and cook for 40 minutes, or until risen and golden brown.
- Meanwhile, make the onion gravy. Put the oil in a pan, add the onions with some seasoning, and cook over medium heat for 10 minutes, or until softened. Reduce the heat slightly, add the sugar, and cook for about another 5 minutes, or until really soft and caramelized. Add the flour, stir to coat, then cook for 2 minutes. Gradually add the broth (stock) a little at a time, stirring constantly to prevent lumps. Once all the broth has been added, cook for 5 minutes, until thickened and bubbling. Add the soy sauce, check the seasoning again, and serve piping hot with the toad in the hole.

CAULIFLOWER CHEESE WITH SPICY TOMATO CHICKPEAS

SERVES 4
PREPARATION TIME: 30 MINUTES
COOKING TIME: 30 MINUTES

FROM THE STORE:
CAULIFLOWER
STRONG CHEDDAR CHEESE

1 CAULIFLOWER, BROKEN INTO FLORETS
2 TABLESPOONS OLIVE OIL, PLUS EXTRA FOR BRUSHING
2 ONIONS, THINLY SLICED
2 CLOVES GARLIC, CHOPPED
5 TABLESPOONS ALL-PURPOSE (PLAIN) FLOUR
GENEROUS 2 CUPS (17 FL OZ/500 ML) MILK
1 TABLESPOON WHOLE GRAIN MUSTARD
1¼ CUPS/5 OZ/150 G GRATED STRONG CHEDDAR CHEESE
SALT AND FRESHLY GROUND BLACK PEPPER

FOR THE SPICY CHICKPEAS
1 × 14-OZ/400-G CAN CHOPPED TOMATOES
1 TABLESPOON SUPERFINE (CASTER) SUGAR
1 TABLESPOON WHITE WINE VINEGAR
1 TABLESPOON SMOKED PAPRIKA
1 TEASPOON CHILI FLAKES
1 × 14-OZ/400-G CAN CHICKPEAS, DRAINED AND RINSED

TIP:
YOU CAN FREEZE CHEESE IF YOU KNOW YOU ARE NOT GOING TO USE THE WHOLE BLOCK IN 1 WEEK. SIMPLY POP IT INTO A CONTAINER, COVER, AND FREEZE UNTIL READY TO USE. YOU CAN EVEN GRATE IT STRAIGHT FROM FROZEN.

We never let any food go to waste; any half eaten vegetable can be cooked and added to the cauliflower cheese mix. Root vegetables or green beans or leaves will add color, taste, and texture to this dish. Be aware of your cooking times; root vegetables will take about 5 minutes longer to cook than the cauliflower.

- Cook the cauliflower in a large pan of boiling salted water for 5 minutes, or until starting to soften. Drain well and set aside.
- Put the pan back on the heat, add the oil, then fry the onions for 10 minutes over medium heat until softened. Add the garlic and fry for another 1 minute. Tip in the flour and stir to coat in the onion mixture. Gradually add the milk, stirring constantly until the sauce is thick and smooth. Remove from the heat, stir in the mustard, half of the cheese, and plenty of seasoning then return the drained cauliflower to the sauce.
- Preheat the oven to 400°F/200°C/Gas mark 6. Tip the cauliflower cheese into a baking dish and sprinkle with the remaining cheese. Bake in the hot oven for 20 minutes, or until golden and bubbling.
- Meanwhile, to make the spicy chickpeas, put all the ingredients into a pan and bring to a boil, then reduce the heat and simmer for 15 minutes, or until the sauce is thick. Season with salt and pepper and serve with the cauliflower cheese.

SMOKED HADDOCK CHOWDER WITH CHIVES AND SOFT POACHED EGG

SERVES 2
PREPARATION TIME: 10 MINUTES
COOKING TIME: 25 MINUTES, PLUS COOLING

FROM THE STORE:
SMOKED HADDOCK
CHIVES

GENEROUS 2 CUPS (17 FL OZ/500 ML) MILK
11 OZ/300 G SMOKED HADDOCK, SKIN AND PIN BONES REMOVED
2 TABLESPOONS OLIVE OIL
1 ONION, FINELY CHOPPED
1 TABLESPOON ALL-PURPOSE (PLAIN) FLOUR
½ BOUILLON (STOCK) CUBE, CRUMBLED
1 TABLESPOON WHITE WINE VINEGAR
2 EGGS
2 TABLESPOONS SNIPPED CHIVES
SALT AND FRESHLY GROUND BLACK PEPPER

This is a really lovely light lunch dish. Smoked fish works perfectly here and the soft poached egg makes the whole thing more luxurious.

- Pour the milk into a medium-size pan. Sit the haddock in the milk, bring to a boil, reduce the heat, and then cook for about 3 minutes, or until the fish is translucent. Remove the fish from the milk with a slotted spoon and transfer to a plate. Break the fish into flakes, removing any remaining bones, and discarding any skin as you go. Allow the milk to cool to room temperature.
- Heat the oil in a pan, add the onion, and fry over medium heat for 8 minutes, or until starting to soften—make sure the onion doesn't take on too much color. Add the flour and bouillon (stock) cube and cook for another minute. Gradually add the room-temperature milk, stirring constantly so that no lumps form. Bring to a gentle simmer and cook for 5 minutes. Reduce the heat, return the fish to the pan with plenty of black pepper and a pinch of salt, and keep warm. Make sure the broth does not boil.
- Meanwhile, divide the vinegar between 2 ramekins or small glasses, swirl the vinegar around the ramekins to coat the sides, and then pour out the excess and discard. Crack an egg into each ramekin. Fill a pan with boiling water from the kettle, and set over medium heat. Stir the boiling water to create a whirlpool, then drop an egg into the center, and cook for 3 minutes for a soft yolk. Remove with a slotted spoon, drain on paper towels, and keep warm while you cook the remaining egg.
- Ladle the broth into 2 warm bowls, drop a poached egg into each dish, and sprinkle with chives. Eat immediately.

PARMESAN SCONES

MAKES 8–10
PREPARATION TIME: 10 MINUTES
COOKING TIME: 15–20 MINUTES, PLUS COOLING

FROM THE STORE:
BUTTER
ITALIAN PARMESAN CHEESE

SCANT 3 CUPS (12 OZ/350 G) ALL-PURPOSE (PLAIN) FLOUR, PLUS EXTRA FOR DUSTING
4 TEASPOONS BAKING POWDER
1 SCANT TEASPOON SMOKED PAPRIKA
½ TEASPOON SALT
¾ STICK (3 OZ/85 G) BUTTER, DICED
1 CUP (2¾ OZ/75 G) FINELY GRATED ITALIAN PARMESAN CHEESE
SCANT 1 CUP (7 FL OZ/200 ML) MILK
FRESHLY GROUND BLACK PEPPER
BUTTER, TO SERVE

TIP:
FOR SPICED SCONES, REPLACE THE PAPRIKA AND PARMESAN CHEESE WITH ½ TEASPOON EACH OF GROUND CORIANDER AND GROUND TURMERIC, AND ½ TEASPOON EACH BASHED CUMIN SEEDS AND BASHED MUSTARD SEEDS.

You can vary the cheese in these scones, or add herbs, such as dried thyme, if you like.

- Preheat the oven to 400°F/200°C/Gas mark 6 and line a baking sheet with parchment (baking) paper.
- Put the flour, baking powder, paprika, and salt into a large bowl, add the butter, then using your hands, rub the butter into the flour until it resembles fine bread crumbs. Stir in all but 2 tablespoons of the cheese and the milk, kneading it very lightly until it forms a dough. Pat the dough out with your hands or a rolling pin on a lightly floured work counter to about ¾ inch/2 cm thick, then, using a 2½-inch/6-cm round cookie cutter, stamp out into circles and put onto the prepared baking sheet. Sprinkle with the remaining cheese, top with a grinding of black pepper, then bake in the hot oven for 15–20 minutes until risen and golden brown. Cool a little, then serve with lots of butter.

FOREST FRUITS BLANCMANGE

SERVES 6
PREPARATION TIME: 10 MINUTES, PLUS 4 HOURS SETTING
COOKING TIME: 20 MINUTES

FROM THE STORE:

FROZEN FOREST FRUITS
GELATIN LEAVES OR POWDERED GELATIN

1 × 14-OZ/400-G BAG OR BOX OF FROZEN FOREST FRUITS, DEFROSTED
GENEROUS ½ CUP (4 OZ/120 G) SUPERFINE (CASTER) SUGAR
6 GELATIN LEAVES OR 1½ SACHETS POWDERED GELATIN
1⅔ CUPS (14 FL OZ/400 ML) MILK

TIP:
YOU CAN REPLACE THE FOREST FRUITS WITH THE JUICE AND ZEST OF 3 ORANGES AND SERVE WITH SOME ORANGE SEGMENTS.

This is a simple, light pudding that's perfect if you want to get ahead by preparing dessert in advance. Blancmange, which is a jelly made from milk instead of water, will sit happily in the refrigerator for a couple of days in the bowl you make it in.

- Put three-quarters of the fruits into a saucepan with the sugar and cook over medium heat for 5 minutes or until the fruit have broken down and released their juices. Remove from the heat, tip into a strainer (sieve) over a clean pan, then press the fruit to squeeze out as much liquid as you can, leaving the pulp and seeds behind. Put the pan containing the fruit juice back over the heat and bring to just below boiling point. Remove from the heat and set aside.
- Meanwhile, put the gelatin in a bowl of cold water and leave to soften for 5 minutes. When the gelatin has softened, squeeze out any excess water and whisk into the warm fruit juice. Stir well until the gelatin has fully dissolved. Alternatively, if using powdered gelatin, put 2 tablespoons water in a small saucepan and sprinkle over the gelatin. Let stand for 5 minutes so that it absorbs the water. Heat over low heat until melted and steaming but not boiling then stir in the warm fruit juice.
- Whisk the milk into the warm fruit juice then pour into a jelly mold or 4¼-cup (34-fl oz/1-liter) ovenproof bowl (pudding basin), or individual glasses and chill for 4 hours, or until set.
- When ready to serve, dip the base of the mold into a bowl of hot water to loosen, run a small knife around the edges and invert onto a plate. Divide among bowls and top with the remaining fruits.

SPANISH FRIED MILK WITH CINNAMON SUGAR

SERVES 4–6
PREPARATION TIME: 10 MINUTES, PLUS 1 HOUR CHILLING
COOKING TIME: 10 MINUTES

FROM THE STORE:
ORANGE
VANILLA BEAN (POD)

⅔ CUP (5 FL OZ/150 ML) OLIVE OIL, FOR FRYING, PLUS EXTRA FOR OILING
GENEROUS 2 CUPS (17 FL OZ/500 ML) MILK, PLUS A SPLASH
GENEROUS ⅓ CUP (2¾ OZ/75 G) SUPERFINE (CASTER) SUGAR
½ TEASPOON GROUND CINNAMON
ZEST OF 1 ORANGE
1 VANILLA BEAN (POD), SEEDS SCRAPED OUT
1½ CUPS (6 OZ/175 G) ALL-PURPOSE (PLAIN) FLOUR
2 EGGS, LIGHTLY BEATEN

FOR THE CINNAMON SUGAR
GENEROUS ⅓ CUP (2¾ OZ/75 G) SUPERFINE (CASTER) SUGAR
2 TEASPOONS GROUND CINNAMON

This is actually fried custard, what could be better? Our favorite thing—fried.

- Oil a small 6 × 6-inch/15 × 15-cm baking sheet or pie dish and line with plastic wrap (clingfilm).
- Heat the milk, sugar, cinnamon, orange zest, vanilla seeds, and generous ¾ cup (3½ oz/100 g) of the flour in a large pan over medium heat, stirring continuously until the mixture comes to the boil. Reduce the heat so that the slow, big bubbles pop on the surface of the milk and the mixture becomes really thick. Pour the custard onto the prepared baking sheet and smooth with the back of a spoon so it is about ¾ inch/2 cm thick. Chill in the refrigerator for at least 1 hour, or until very firm.
- Put the remaining flour and the eggs into 2 separate bowls. Cut the chilled custard into ¾-inch/2-cm squares and roll each cube in the flour, dust off any excess, then dip each cube into the egg then back into the flour until coated. Place the coated squares on a plate.
- To make the cinnamon sugar, mix the sugar and cinnamon together in a wide bowl and set aside.
- Heat the oil in a small skillet (frying pan) over medium heat. When the oil is hot, add the custard squares in batches, and fry for 1–2 minutes, or until golden. Remove with a slotted spoon and drain on paper towels.
- Toss the squares in the cinnamon sugar and serve hot.

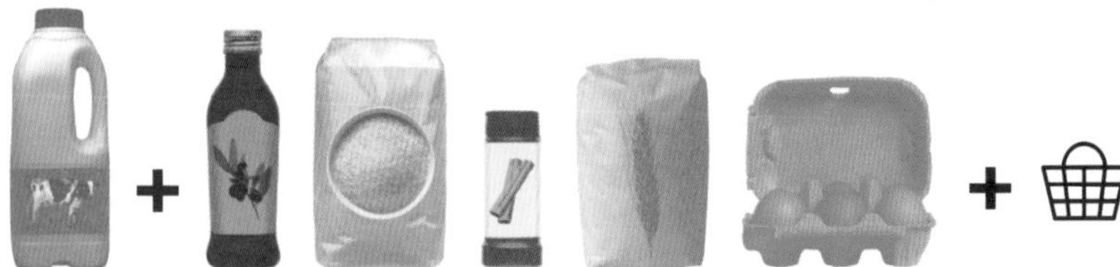

INDEX

NOTES ON THE RECIPES

Butter should always be unsalted, unless otherwise specified.

All herbs are dried, unless otherwise specified.

Eggs and individual vegetables and fruits, such as onions and apples, are assumed to be medium, unless otherwise specified.

All milk is whole (full-fat) milk, unless otherwise specified.

All salt is sea salt flakes, unless otherwise specified.

Chickpeas are also known as garbanzo beans.

Cooking times are for guidance only, as individual ovens vary. If using a convection (fan) oven, follow the manufacturer's instructions concerning oven temperatures.

Exercise a high level of caution when following recipes involving any potentially hazardous activity, including the use of high temperatures, open flames, and when deep-frying. In particular, when deep-frying, add food carefully to avoid splashing, wear long sleeves, and never leave the pan unattended.

Some recipes include raw or very lightly cooked eggs, meat, or fish, and fermented products. These should be avoided by the elderly, infants, pregnant women, convalescents, and anyone with an impaired immune system.

When no quantity is specified, for example of oils, salts, and herbs used for finishing dishes or for deep frying, quantities are discretionary and flexible.

Both metric and imperial measures are used in this book. Follow one set of measurements throughout, not a mixture, as they are not interchangeable.

All spoon and cup measurements are level, unless otherwise stated. 1 teaspoon = 5 ml; 1 tablespoon = 15 ml.

Australian standard tablespoons are 20 ml, so Australian readers are advised to use 3 teaspoons in place of 1 tablespoon when measuring small quantities.

ABOUT THE AUTHORS AND ACKNOWLEDGEMENTS

ABOUT THE AUTHORS

Eve O'Sullivan is a London-based food writer, cookbook author, food stylist, and editor of Cooked.com. She is a regular columnist for Guardian Cook, for which she writes the weekly Readers' Recipe Swap. She has written for magazines such as *Olive*, *Delicious*, and *Harper's Bazaar* online, and gives Guardian Masterclasses in food styling, blogging, and recipe writing.

Rosie Reynolds is a London-based food stylist, recipe writer, and developer. Having trained at Leiths School of Food and Wine, she went on to work for *BBC Good Food* and *Olive* magazines in London. She has styled many books, including Ella Woodward's *Deliciously Ella*, and writes recipes and food styles for magazines such as *Good Food*, *Olive*, *Waitrose Kitchen* and *Stella*, as well as the *Guardian*, the *Independent Review* and *Australian Sunday Life*. She also gives Guardian Masterclasses in food styling and recipe writing.

ACKNOWLEDGEMENTS

One thing that Eve and I share is our love of work that doesn't feel like work at all. We got lucky in our pursuit of this the day we sent our book proposal to Phaidon. Little did we know we'd get to meet, and later work with, the wonderful Ellie Smith. From the start we laughed our heads off at nothing at all and thoroughly enjoyed "working" with Ellie. Thank you for loving our idea and for making it into this fabulous book. And Sophie Hodgkin, with your fine toothcomb and attention to detail, you are a calm beauty with graceful persistence. To work with one author who likes work not to feel like work is probably painful enough, but two of us with our giggling fits and rambling tales must have been a nightmare at times. We are eternally grateful for your patience and commitment to our book. We love it.

Thank you to Julia Hasting for such a beautiful design, to Michael Wallace and João Mota for all your art working help, and to everyone at Phaidon for such a great book. We are both very proud.

We would like to thank Rachel Vere, a wonderful stylist and our great friend, for begging, borrowing, and sourcing such beautiful props. Your vision is amazing and you do everything with so much passion and always with such an infectious smile. You helped us so much, right from the start, and we are so happy that we got a dose of your talent into our book.

Andy Sewell, thank you for the beautiful photos and for being such a keen taster on the shoot. It was lovely to work with you.

The Price family, especially Kim, thank you for welcoming us into your home everyday. You, Jasper, and Penny turned what could have been a stressful time into a joyous two weeks filled with coloring in, drawing, and general silliness.

From Eve:
I still can't believe I've been able to do this project, but I know it simply would not have happened had not *Olive* magazine hired me a few years ago. Thank you to all the amazing people I've worked with there, but especially to Janine Ratcliffe—I could not have made the next step without your wisdom and encouragement.

To everyone at Guardian Cook, thank you so much for letting me hop on board. From my first day to now it's been a genuine dream come true. Thank you for taking a chance on me Nell.

Working with someone who truly encourages you to be yourself, both in real life and on a plate, is a rare privilege; Rosie, it's been an absolute joy, and I'm as proud of our book as I am to count you as a dear friend.

I owe a huge debt of gratitude to my family, who have somehow managed to put up with the botched timings, burnt dinners, and enormous portions that have come with my endless enthusiasm for learning more about the thing I love. Special thanks to my mother-in-law, Deirdre, for being such a willing recipe tester, and of course my incredible Mum, Mary. I simply don't know where I would be without you.

Finally, Davo, thank you for not only putting up with me, but for approaching everything I've cooked for you with an empty belly, an honest heart, and an open mind. You are the reason I always want to do better.

From Rosie:
I would like to thank all those people who have helped me achieve this dream, who embraced me and encouraged me to be myself: my teachers at Leiths Cookery School; all at BBC Good Food, especially Barney Desmazery; the Guardian Cook team, your generosity and trust is amazing; all the wonderful publishers and magazines who allowed me to do what I love doing so much and who gave me the confidence to even consider writing a book.

The wonderful Eve O you're a delight and this has been so much fun—thank you—let's do it again soon.

Finally, thank you Eileen for your generosity and to my lovely Mum and Dad, Woodsy and Bren, you're the kindest, most wonderful people I know. This is for you (to use, not for decoration).

PHAIDON PRESS LIMITED
REGENT'S WHARF
ALL SAINTS STREET
LONDON N1 9PA

PHAIDON PRESS INC.
65 BLEECKER STREET
NEW YORK, NY 10012
PHAIDON.COM

FIRST PUBLISHED 2016

ISBN 978 0 7148 7127 1

A CIP CATALOGUE RECORD FOR THIS BOOK IS AVAILABLE FROM THE BRITISH LIBRARY.

COMMISSIONING EDITOR: ELLIE SMITH
PROJECT EDITOR: SOPHIE HODGKIN
PRODUCTION CONTROLLER: REBECCA PRICE

DESIGNED BY JULIA HASTING
ARTWORKED BY MICHAEL WALLACE
RECIPE PHOTOGRAPHY BY ANDY SEWELL
FOOD STYLING BY EVE O'SULLIVAN AND ROSIE REYNOLDS
PROP STYING BY RACHEL VERE
BASKET ICON BY JOEL AVERY, FROM THENOUNPROJECT.COM

THE PUBLISHER WOULD LIKE TO THANK ANOTHER COUNTRY, BERT AND MAY, CLARE CHURLY, CLOTH HOUSE, FIRED EARTH, JANE ELLIS, LAURA LEA DESIGN, LUCAS LICCINI, ISOBEL MCLEAN, JOÃO MOTA, KATHY STEER, SUSAN SPAULL, HANS STOFREGEN, AND RACHEL VERE FOR THEIR CONTRIBUTIONS TO THE BOOK.

PRINTED IN CHINA